Glendale College
Library

CHILD CARE:
A COMPREHENSIVE GUIDE

Philosophy, Programs and Practices
for the Creation of Quality Service for Children

A SERIES

edited by

Stevanne Auerbach, Ph.D.

with

James A. Rivaldo

VOLUME I

Subsequent Volumes in this series include:

Volume II. MODEL PROGRAMS AND THEIR COMPONENTS
Experiences from across the country and views of health, mental health, and education specialists.

Volume III. CREATIVE CENTERS AND HOMES
Approaches to the design and implementation of the child's environment, and a focus on infant care and family day care homes.

Volume IV. SPECIAL NEEDS AND SERVICES
Methods for working with young children who are handicapped, abused, or having other special problems, and with an emphasis on parents, minority groups, and responsive programs.

RATIONALE FOR CHILD CARE SERVICES: PROGRAMS vs. POLITICS

VOLUME ONE
in the series
CHILD CARE:
A COMPREHENSIVE GUIDE

Edited by
Stevanne Auerbach, Ph.D.
with
James A. Rivaldo

Foreword by
Senator Walter F. Mondale
Chairman, U.S. Senate Subcommittee
on Children and Youth

HUMAN SCIENCES PRESS, INC. ● NEW YORK
A division of Behavioral Publications, Inc.

Library of Congress Catalog Number 74-11877
ISBN: 0-87705-218-2

Published by Human Sciences Press, a division
of Behavioral Publications, Inc.
72 Fifth Avenue
New York, New York 10011

Printed in the United States of America
56789 98765432

Library of Congress Cataloging in Publication Data

Auerbach, Stevanne.
    Rationale for child care services—programs vs. politics.
    (Their Child care—a comprehensive guide; v. 1)
    Bibliography: p.
    1. Day care centers—United States—Addresses,
essay, lectures. 2. Child welfare—United States—
Addresses, essays, lectures. I. Rivaldo, James A.,
joint author. II. Title.
HV741.A94 vol. 1 [HV854] 362.7'08s [362.7'1] 74-11877

For the children now in child care in America,
the children who are waiting,
and to all who can respond to them.

GENERAL PREFACE

Years of involvement in education and day care have exposed me to the full range of issues involved in planning, establishing, maintaining, and evaluating ongoing children's programs. The primary source of my familiarity with child care issues has been direct, personal contact with literally hundreds of people actively involved in all aspects of child care, from developmental education theorists to day care center workers, parents, and children.

One nearly universal problem encountered by people working in the child care movement has been the difficulty of communicating with and coordinating the efforts of all the essential components of a comprehensive child care program. In preparing this *Guide* I solicited contributions from people who have participated in various ways in defining the goals of day care programs, generating nationwide and community support for day care programs, starting day care centers in their communities and administering and teaching in ongoing programs. Many of the contributors have already earned recognition for their efforts. Many others have never before been published, but bring a wealth of practical knowledge and personal insight into the daily operations of day care centers.

As new recruits enter the child care movement I hope they will join many others who are eager to put their time and effort to work not in endless theoretical or political debate, but in providing warm, cheerful places and stimulating opportunities for young children. I hope the information contained in this series will find practical application by concerned and committed people eager to provide the means for children to reach their fullest potential within the context of more economically and psychologically secure families served by improved day care systems throughout the nation.

Stevanne Auerbach
San Francisco, California
September, 1974

CONTENTS

FOREWORD

During my ten years in the Senate, I have probably devoted as much of my time working with the problems of children as on any other issue. I have seen many ways in which public and private programs have helped children, and many other ways in which they can and should help them. But as good as some of our public and private institutions can be—and we have some excellent schools and day care programs—it has become increasingly clear to me that there is just no substitute for a healthy family— nothing else that can give a child as much love, support, confidence, motivation or feelings of self-worth and self-respect.

Yet, it is also clear that we tend to take families for granted, seldom recognizing the pressures they are experiencing. That is why the Senate Subcommittee on Children and Youth, which I am privileged to chair, began hearings last year concerning the trends and pressures affecting American families. Some of the major findings of those hearings underscored the increasing need for family-oriented child care services.

One of those findings concerned the tremendous increase in the number of working mothers, especially among the rapidly increasing number of single parent families:

—In 1971, 43 percent of the nation's mothers worked outside the home, compared to only 18 percent in 1948.

—One out of every three mothers with preschool children is working today, compared to one out of eight in 1948.

—Thirteen percent of all children—some 8.3 million—are living in single parent families, and 65 percent of these parents are working.

—Yet, there are only about 700,000 spaces in licensed day care centers to serve the six million preschool children whose mothers work.

Some of these children are receiving adequate care while their mothers work, but many are not. Many are left in understaffed day care centers, and many others are left alone to look after themselves, because that is all their parents can afford.

Our hearings on the American families revealed a second striking trend that has paralleled the dramatic increase of working mothers. Over the past several decades, America has experienced the virtual disappearance of the extended family. Testimony showed that at the turn of the century, for example, 50 percent of the homes in Boston contained parents, their children, and at least one other adult—a grandparent, an aunt, or other relative. The comparable figure today is about 4 percent. This is representative of the decline in extended families nationally. And this has meant a tremendous decrease in the availability of relatives to look after children when both mother and father are working.

These trends and pressures help explain why the 1970 White House Conference on Children, composed of a broad cross-section of over 4,000 delegates representing every walk of life across the nation, identified as its number one priority among children's services the provision of "comprehensive family-oriented development programs including health services, day care and early childhood education." That Conference kindled new hopes for and commitment to a decade of progress in meeting the ever-increasing needs of America's families. The Congress responded by passing the Comprehensive Child Development Act of 1971, which I sponsored in the Senate, but President Nixon vetoed the bill.

Despite the Administration's insensitivity to the need for expanded child and family services, some promising efforts have been undertaken in communities throughout the United States. But for every story of local initiative and success one hears many others of frustration and disappointment, largely because the Federal Government has not committed sufficient resources or assistance to support efforts designed to expand and upgrade the quality of child care available.

The effort to assure that sufficient resources become available to support child and family services continues. As of this writing, Congress is considering the Child and Family Services Act of 1974, which I have sponsored in the Senate with 23 co-sponsors, and Representative Brademas has sponsored in the House of Representatives with over 50 co-sponsors. We have already begun joint Senate-House hearings on the measure. This legislation is a revised version of the vetoed bill. It authorizes a wide variety of child and family services—on a totally voluntary basis—including prenatal care, nutrition assistance, part-day programs like Head Start, after-school or full-day developmental day care for children of working mothers, in-the-home tutoring, early medical screening and treatment to detect and remedy handicapping conditions, and classes for parents and prospective parents.

The series of articles in *Child Care: A Comprehensive Guide*, compiled and edited by Dr. Stevanne Auerbach, of which this is the first volume, makes a significant contribution toward clarifying the issues in child care and making it possible for those interested to deal with these problems with intelligence and sensitivity. It can contribute to the kind of public understanding and discussion that those of us involved in the policy process are anxious to encourage.

The first volume sets forth the history of child care in America and explores many of the major issues in the field today. The contributors to this volume have distinguished themselves in their efforts on behalf of children, and their years of experience and insight provide a useful introduction to child care and set the stage for the more practically oriented volumes that follow.

Senator Walter F. Mondale
Chairman, Subcommittee on
Children and Youth
September, 1974

INTRODUCTION

THE CHALLENGE

Millions of Americans, professionals and laymen alike, have focused their attention increasingly on the question of how best to meet the needs of children in a technological and democratic society. Child development and child care specialists agree that much remains to be done to ensure that all children in the United States are provided with the best possible nurturing environment. Research has amply demonstrated that a child's early years are formative, critical years of growth, and that these years require greater attention and expansion of child care services.

Federal legislation passed during the 1960's, including Head Start and Title IV-A amendments to the Social Security Act, took the first steps toward recognizing the special needs of young children, particularly children from poverty-level or single-parent families. The 1970 White House Conference on Children, which convened, it seemed, with the support of the Administration, outlined unmet needs in child care. The movement suffered a disappointing setback, however, as the federal government, through former President Nixon's veto of the Comprehensive Child Care Act of 1970, indicated its unwilling-ness to proceed with the national support needed for a high quality educational and developmental child care sys-tem.

Thus observers saw a decrease not only in attention to the needs of young children, but also in critically needed funds for the expansion and improvement of children's programs. This guide addresses itself to the growing gap between human needs and human services and responds with practical and realistic recommendations. The families that do not have adequate child care now cannot afford to wait for the 1980 White House Conference on Children to obtain a national commitment and response to their child care needs.

Day care centers and homes are not a new idea. From earliest colonial days through World War II to the present, social organizations and branches of the local, state and federal governments have provided some funds for facilities and programs for the care of preschool children outside their homes. The rate of progress in child care, however, has not kept pace with the rate of economic and technological progress and social change in this na-tion. Educators and child care specialists have drawn the blueprints and developed many pilot programs. All they need is public attention, support and funding to turn the dream of preschool educational and developmental op-portunities into reality.

Child Care: A Comprehensive Guide addresses itself to the problems, concerns and issues of the field of early childhood and child care. Experts in various aspects of child care are given the opportunity to share their know-ledge and insights with those concerned students, parents and professionals eager to take the initiative in bringing improved child care programs to their own communities.

Articles have appeared almost daily in newspapers throughout the country detailing the struggles to develop funding for existing and proposed child care programs.

Despite the efforts organizations and individuals have made to spur their state and federal legislators to positive action, the news from state capitals and Washington D.C. usually brings threats of cutbacks and discontinuance. Although progress is being made every day, working and concerned parents have not yet sufficiently organized themselves into lobbies that are potent and effective enough to represent children's interests in state and federal legislatures. Working mothers have not yet spoken out with the unity and forcefulness that commands the continued attention of legislatures and policy makers. Each year's delay means that hundreds of thousands of young children have missed out for the rest of their lives on what perhaps might have been the most significant single boost that would enable them to attain their fullest intellectual, social and economic potential.

Although the general public has the impression that child care programs are aimed primarily at welfare or poverty-level families, these programs hold enormous potential benefit for families at every socioeconomic level. Welfare mothers benefit from child care in that they are freed to seek and maintain employment and can thus help their families attain economic independence. Other skilled and educated women who would otherwise see their professional training and talents wasted can, with the support of child care services, make significant contributions to society. Most importantly, the children in quality child care programs benefit from the intellectual and social stimulation provided.

Since the responsibility for initiating child care programs has shifted, at least temporarily, to state and local communities, many child care advocates find themselves battling against inevitable mistakes, community apathy, misunderstandings and misinformation. As a result, progress is often painfully slow and many otherwise energetic and committed persons find themselves disheartened and disillusioned.

Child Care: A Comprehensive Guide is designed to relieve the student and the child care planner and organizer of some of these sources of frustration and delay. Each contribution was selected on the ground that the author's practical experiences in child care programs would be of value to persons throughout the country who are active in the child care movement. The authors' knowledge and insights, taken as a whole, outline a course of action that ranges from organizing a community, to designing a child care facility, through developing and evaluating different components of child care programs to meet the needs of individual children in any given community. Each volume concentrates on specific areas, and the collection as a whole will span a broad spectrum of historical and programmatic considerations, dating from the past to the trends of the late 60's and early 70's.

The need for child care services has more than doubled in the past ten years, not only because of the increase in the number of young children, but also because an increasingly higher percentage of women are joining the labor force. Women are ascribing greater importance to their own efforts toward economic independence. The definition of a good mother is no longer delineated by the total amount of time, and presumably attention, a woman devotes to housework and to being with her children. Women have taken on a larger role in their communities, and society has benefited enormously from their talents and resources. However, society has not yet responded by providing assistance to mothers struggling to manage their sometimes conflicting resvonsibilities. Child care programs sensitively attuned to the subtle human needs of young children and their working parents can increase tremendously the potential contributions children and women alike can make to society.

Child care programs operating in different locations vary considerably in their size, the number of children served, the quality of facilities and the extent of training of their staff. Most programs are regulated by combinations of local, state and federal requirements, which make rules on everything from building codes, staff certification and training and family eligibility to funding sources. In addition, the mechanisms and effectiveness of licensing and enforcing agencies vary widely. Consequently, the possibilities of confusion and inefficiency are vast and present formidable challenges to anyone attempting to start a program. The problems of dealing with the seemingly endless paperwork in the proper sequence are augmented by the problems of dealing with the vicissitudes of community opinion and government attitudes toward funding, which vary from year to year.

Licensed quality child care is an expensive proposition, with its requirements for high staff/child ratios, specially built facilities and numerous support agencies and services. The most likely potential and current users of child care usually are those least able to afford the costs of these services. Child care should rightfully be viewed as a logical extension of the social service and educational system already reaching children of diverse socioeconomic backgrounds in their most receptive and critical developmental years. Instead, however, a society wary of expensive new social welfare programs has lumped it with confusing issues such as guaranteed annual income and various national health or welfare reform plans, and with such emotionally charged issues as abortion and women's liberation.

So as one group of child care advocates takes on the task of informing the public and gathering their support, another group, those most directly affected, working mothers with little time and energy to deal even with their everyday problems, struggle on their own to arrange child care. Rarely do they encounter a program that gains their confidence as a permanent solution. Mothers must often endure either the expense and uncertainty of a series of sitters, or child care centers or homes which, either through inadequate funding or some other deficiency, do not meet mother's needs and expectations. Difficulties relating to location, transportation, daily schedule, program content, cost and the insensitivity of staff to ethnic tradition and language are some of the problems parents have mentioned.

Child care professionals thus find themselves in the middle of three powerful and demanding forces. The first force can broadly be classified as the bureaucracy, which establishes and administers child care policy codes and regulations, and which appropriates and administers funds. The second force is the general public, whose awareness of and support for the purposes of child care can be crucial to the success of a program. And the third element is the child care consumer, who brings a unique set of personal considerations, which must be dealt with sensitively and intelligently in order for the program to succeed.

Persons wishing to involve themselves in child care, whether as community organizers, program administrators and staff, or as concerned and informed parents, must be aware of the total unmet need and recognize how they can prepare themselves for dealing with the complexities of the movement.

THE PURPOSE

The availability or lack of child care services often determines whether millions of mothers of young children can work or attend school. These services do not meet the human need of families if they merely provide places to park children for the day. Decades of research have shown beyond question that the kind of attention children receive in their preschool years has long-range effects. It is thus vital that children in child care programs experience attractive and stimulating environments, warm and consistent attention by staff members, and opportunities to socialize, express themselves and exercise their bodies. Beyond these basic considerations, the child care program should not squander the opportunity to provide children with a challenging educational component that encourages each individual to develop his/her natural abilities at a natural pace.

The contributors to the *Guide* point out ways in which many different people can share and contribute to service in child care. Success will come when parents, professionals and other community members can work together in a combined, systematic attack on the problems that have frustrated so many families for so long. The articles that appear in the *Guide* provide a course of action.

The plan for this *Guide* evolved from my own experiences as an educator, a program specialist in the United States Office of Education and Office of Economic Opportunity and, perhaps most importantly, as a working mother trying to provide for the many needs of my young daughter. I soon found that many of my co-workers shared the same problems as they worked and raised a family at the same time.

I decided to mobilize the resources of the federal government to create a center for the employees of HEW, of which my own department was a part. This child care center would serve, first as a multi-faceted example of an employer meeting the needs of its workers; next as an educational and social agency developing a program for the care and education of preschool children; and simultaneously, as a linkage for the child development specialists and educators working in the Department of Health, Education and Welfare and elsewhere in the nation.

After a long and difficult struggle, the centers at HEW and OEO finally opened. My duties as a program specialist in day care at OEO enabled me to travel throughout the United States visiting, evaluating, planning and developing strategies for funding and improving child care programs. I brought back to Washington word of the problems I encountered everywhere, descriptions of the ambitious attempts people were making to solve these problems and the anticipation of the expected new legislation and funds to create better care.

My efforts in Washington were aimed at formulating a national policy on day care and developing a strategy for its implementation. As an active participant in the decennial White House Conference on Children in 1970, I felt for the first time that the nation was making great strides toward that goal. I soon learned otherwise, however, as the urgent bipartisan pleas for increased child care support went unheeded by the White House and the Bureau of the Budget. As the consultant to the Day Care Forum of the Conference, I saw firsthand how the most convincing information, striking dedication and honest, programmatic proposals can be totally disregarded by those in power on policy-making levels. The health and well-being of young children is a resource as easily depleted as air, water and energy, but unfortunately mothers and children are not organized with the same forcefulness as corporations, labor unions, veterans' associations and other special interest groups that wield considerable influence in Washington.

Around this time I moved to San Francisco, feeling that I could be most effective there in advancing the cause of child care as I completed work toward a doctorate in child development. The study I undertook there of the needs and expectations of child care users grew eventually into this *Guide*, which is an outgrowth of my contact with those active nationally in the child care movement.

Child Care: A Comprehensive Guide is designed as a practical step toward the improvement and expansion of child care services throughout the country. The objective of each of the volumes is to bring information on the ingredients of successful child care programs to those working on behalf of children. The series includes practical ideas for incorporation into new or ongoing programs.

Additionally, the *Guide* is aimed at encouraging and informing those studying to become professionals in child care. Professionals in allied health, education and social services will perhaps discover ways of contributing their knowledge and talents to the expansion of child care services. Citizens and policymakers will, I hope, find the information they need to reassign child care programs to a higher priority, and to establish priorities within the goal of expanded child care services.

In the first volume of the series, the historical background and current status of child care services is outlined by such nationally known experts as Mary Keyserling, Therese Lansburgh, Dorothy Hewes, Jeanada Nolan and Gertrude Hoffman. Practical suggestions regarding organizing lobbies for children or organizing and coordinating community resources and planning and starting child care programs and centers are advanced by Glen Nimnicht, Jule Sugarman, William Pierce and Elizabeth Haas. The problems of the families and rationale for day care is presented by Stevanne Auerbach, as editor and parent-professional.

In later volumes, topics of importance will be presented by Helen Gordon, Kay Martin, Mary Millman, June Sale and Jean Berman, as they relate experiences in planning and developing successful programs in different parts of the country. Designing the structure and organizing the space inside and outside a child care facility will be discussed by Fred Osmon, Jay Beckwith, Valerie Annixter, Allison Kuhn and Gloria Weissberg.

The needs of children in child care programs in general, and particularly of children from different backgrounds and abilities, are presented by Ann Peters, Bettye Caldwell, Marilyn Humes, Lottie Rosen, Dorothy Shack, Oscar Uribe, Jim Johnson, Mila Pascual, Rod Auyang, Elsa Ten Broeck, Carol Ann Winfrey, Judith Lewis and Gloria Powell. Special areas are also covered by Bertha Addison, Fran Lewis, Keith Alward, Don Safran, James Levine, and others.

Children deserve the best possible environment to foster their growth and development. Each child has his/her own unique patterns for growing. However, children depend entirely on adults to provide the environment they need to grow to their fullest potential. This *Guide* contains pertinent information and insight to assist adults responsible for planning, implementing and improving child care programs.

The care of preschool children involves many sensitive and complex issues. A child care program is not just an educational program, nor is it simply a convenience for its users. Child care programs, in order truly to be an extension and supplement to the child's family life, must make the extra effort to seek out the active interest, support and participation of parents. In order to do so, child care planners and organizers must consider at every step the vast array of personal situations and human needs of child care users.

Once local communities have pooled their energy and resources to undertake solutions to their own problems, perhaps then the federal government will play a larger role in offering guidance and funding assistance to ongoing local programs. The first steps must be taken by dedicated and informed persons, aware of the needs of their communities, and eager to wield their influence on behalf of children. I hope that *Child Care: A Comprehensive Guide* will contribute to this long-overdue movement and support the efforts being made on behalf of child care throughout the United States.

—S. A.

PREFACE TO VOLUME I

Few areas of public policy have generated as much controversy as the issues involved in forging a national commitment to child care services for preschool children. While the debates rage in testimony before federal, state and local legislators, many local organizations and energetic individuals have pushed ahead with their own efforts to bring child care to their communities.

The articles in this first volume of *Child Care: A Comprehensive Guide* present an introduction to the major concerns in child care, defining the nature and extent of the need, outlining the history of child care, suggesting essential components of comprehensive programs and describing the procedures for organizing into citizens' lobbies and child care organizations.

Mary Keyserling reports on a 1971-72 study of day care needs and services in 77 cities, reaching the general conclusion that need far outstrips availability. Her article also traces the course of recent federal child care legislation.

Therese Lansburgh examines the issues in day care from the perspectives of the children, their parents and the government. She defines areas of concern and responsibility in the expansion of day care services.

Dorothy Hewes outlines the history of child rearing from medieval days, setting forth the evolution of attitudes toward children up until the beginning of the twentieth century.

Jeanada Nolan discusses the history of child care in California, the only state to continue to support day care when federal funding ceased following World War II.

Gertrude Hoffman describes the needs of children for various types of child care programs, emphasizing the necessity of providing a secure, warm environment. She also examines the dimensions of national day care needs, the status of legislation and funding sources, and the special role physicians should undertake in child care programs.

Jule Sugarman draws on his vast experience in establishing and administering a wide variety of social service programs in a paper outlining step-by-step the procedure for setting up a comprehensive child care program with government funding.

William Pierce explores private, proprietary day care franchises and describes why, in the face of such pressing need, private enterprise has not been able to establish itself in the field.

Glen Nimnicht sets forth the basic requirements of a comprehensive child care system and discusses the strengths and weaknesses of various arrangements and programs.

Elizabeth Haas describes the procedures needed for establishing citizens' lobbies to promote the interests of children in state and federal legislatures.

Stevanne Auerbach reports on her 1971-73 study, *Parents and Child Care: A Report on Child Care Consumers in San Francisco.* Based on surveys and interviews the study gives insight into the reasons why mothers need increased child care services, the problems they have in locating suitable programs for their children and the difficulties they face in meeting the dual responsibilities of employment and raising a family. In the course of her interviews with mothers, Dr. Auerbach frequently encountered the sentiment that mothers were rarely consulted in policy making and administration of child care programs. Her study provided mothers with the opportunity to articulate their expectations regarding child care, quantify their responses and set forth a statement of priorities as addressed by the other authors in the series.

ACKNOWLEDGMENTS

The editor wishes to acknowledge the following publications or organizations for permission to include the articles in this volume:

Harvard University Publication, *Inequality in Education* (No. 13, Dec. 1972) for "The Magnitude of Day Care Needs" by Mary Dublin Keyserling (updated August 1974).

The Child Welfare League for "Profiting from Day Care" by William L. Pierce.

The Woman Physician of the American Women's Medical Association for "The Day Care World of Children" by Gertrude L. Hoffman.

Day Care and Early Education for "What Parents Want from Day Care" by Stevanne Auerbach.

In addition the editor would like to thank Mr. James A. Rivaldo for his outstanding editorial assistance in the preparation of this series; Kathy Loos and Sarah Ingle for their secretarial services; David, Daniel and Nancy Fink and Amy Auerbach, my four children who were supportive during its development; and especially my husband, Dr. Donald L. Fink, who shares the view that we can create high quality child care services for all children. And to all of the generous and talented authors who were willing to share their wisdom and experience with you, the reader, I thank you for your participation and contribution to this effort.

CONTRIBUTORS TO VOLUME I

STEVANNE AUERBACH. Editor of *Child Care: A Comprehensive Guide* and a consultant in education and child care, Stevanne Auerbach completed doctoral studies in child development with the Union Graduate School of the Union of Experimenting Colleges and Universities in September, 1973. She has been an intern in child development with Dr. Glen P. Nimnicht at the Far West Laboratory for Educational Research and Development and resides now in San Francisco. From 1968 to 1971, she served as program specialist in Education and Day Care with the Office of Education, U.S. Department of Health, Education and Welfare and the Office of Economic Opportunity. She was the staff consultant to the Day Care Forum of the 1970 White House Conference on Children. While at HEW, after testifying in 1969 on the "Need for Day Care Services for Federal Employees" to the Select Subcommittee of the Education and Labor Committee, she helped to establish the first day care centers at HEW, OE and OEO.

ELIZABETH HAAS. A consultant on federal, state and local legislation, Elizabeth Haas has a wide range of experience in early childhood education and child care program development. Following three years of teaching in public elementary schools, Ms. Haas moved to the Office of Child Development, Department of Health, Education and Welfare in Washington, D.C., and served as a liaison with federal agencies to coordinate early childhood and youth programs. From there she moved to the Human Resources Administration in New York City, where she served as a liaison for various social and education programs. Most recently she has worked with the childhood and government project as a law student at the University of California, Berkeley, and a member of the board of the California Children's Lobby.

DOROTHY HEWES. An authority on the development of early childhood education, Dr. Hewes is currently Associate Professor in the School of Family Studies at San Diego State University and is an active member of the National Association for the Education of Young Children. She has co-authored *Early Childhood Education: A Workbook for Administrators* and *Early Childhood Education: Its First Century in California.*

GERTRUDE L. HOFFMAN. Ms. Hoffman, educator and social worker, is Program Specialist on Day Care Services, Office of Service Development, Community Services Administration, Social and Rehabilitation Service, Department of Health, Education and Welfare, Washington, D.C. She has authored a variety of publications on day care, recently on school age child care.

MARY DUBLIN KEYSERLING. Former director of the Women's Bureau, U.S. Department of Labor, Ms. Keyserling directed a study on day care for the National Council of Jewish Women, and is the author of its report *Windows on*

Day Care. She also has authored *New York City Child Care Programs—Challenges Ahead*, sponsored by the Day Care Council of New York, Inc. Since 1972, Ms. Keyserling has been the director of Project Action Now for Children and Youth. Currently president of the National Day Care Association, she resides in Washington, D.C.

THERESE W. LANSBURGH. During her tenure as president of the Day Care and Child Development Council of America, Therese Lansburgh initiated the groundwork for formation of a day care constituency. Ms. Lansburgh served as vice chairperson of the Developmental Child Care Forum of the 1970 White House Conference on Children and has continued to work toward implementing the recommendations of the Forum. As a direct result of these responsibilities, Ms. Lansburgh was active in the formation of the Children's Lobby and now serves as president of the Maryland Committee for the Day Care of Children.

GLEN P. NIMNICHT. Formerly the program director of Education Beginning at Age Three, which included the Responsive and Parent Toy Lending Library Programs of the Far West Laboratory for Educational Research and Development, Dr. Nimnicht also has consulted with the Education Commission of the States and is now associated with the Early Childhood Programs of Nova University in Florida. Dr. Nimnicht's experience in education also includes his service as a teacher, principal and superintendent of schools in Wyoming and California, and as a professor of education at Colorado State College, where he directed, under a Ford Foundation grant, an Experimental Project in Teacher Education. Between 1964 and 1967 Dr. Nimnicht directed the New Nursery School, an experimental school for three - and four-year-old children from low-income families.

JEANADA H. NOLAN. Formerly an assistant program manager for early childhood education in the California State Department of Education, Jeanada Nolan has had many years of experience in a broad range of education and social welfare responsibilities, including ten years spent supervising adoptions, boarding homes, institutions and day care; and seventeen years as a teacher and coordinator of Parent and Preschool Education for the Sacramento, California public school system and for Head Start programs. Ms. Nolan also has served on the Governor's Advisory Committee on Children and Youth and has been a lecturer and discussion leader at the University of California.

WILLIAM L. PIERCE. Currently the child care consultant for the Child Welfare League of America, William Pierce was formerly director of the League's Washington Office. Mr. Pierce joined the League in June, 1970, to direct a foundation-funded study of the expansion of day care in the United States. Prior to joining the League, Pierce was associate director of the Day Care and Child Development Council of America, a national voluntary organization based in Washington. Mr. Pierce has also gained experience in government from having served three years with the Office of Economic Opportunity and as the director of a statewide Neighborhood Youth Corps project.

JULE M. SUGARMAN. Jule M. Sugarman's twenty-two-year career in public service has exposed him to an extraordinary variety of service programs in Washington, D.C., New York City and Atlanta, Ga., as administrator of human resources programs. In the course of his service with the United States government in the Bureau of the Budget, Bureau of Prisons, Department of State, Office of Economic Opportunity and in the Department of Health, Education and Welfare, as well as in his present position, Mr. Sugarman has assumed major leadership responsibility including creation of the Head Start program, creation of the Office of Child Development, founding of the Children's Lobby and in establishing the Community Co-ordinated Child Care Program.

Chapter One

THE MAGNITUDE OF DAY CARE NEED

Mary Dublin Keyserling

The challenge of day care needs is vital to us all. Our children are our future, and deserve the very best we can provide for their growth and development. Yet millions of our children today are denied the chance to realize their potentials because they lack the developmental opportunities that should be their birthright.

Two groups of children need developmental day care urgently. The first group is children of employed mothers who cannot arrange for satisfactory care for them at home. The second group is those whose families are economically deprived, whose mothers are not now working and who lack the kind of preschool developmental opportunities on a part-day basis which would give them an equal start with more privileged children.

One of the most dramatic social changes in recent decades has been the rapid increase in the employment of women. Thirty-six and one-half million women are in the labor force today. While the number of all working women has increased nearly three-fold since 1940, the number of working mothers has increased nearly nine-fold, and now exceeds thirteen million. More than half of all mothers

1

with children aged six to seventeen are job holders. More than one third of all mothers with children under the age of six, totalling nearly five million women, are workers, and have taken jobs for compelling economic reasons. They are faced with the difficult problem of obtaining adequate care for their children while they are away from home. There are now more than six million children under the age of six whose mothers are in the labor force.

A survey made in the mid-1960's by the Women's Bureau (U.S. Department of Labor) and the Children's Bureau (HEW) clearly revealed that a large proportion of the children of working mothers are inadequately cared for while their mothers are at work. (All available evidence indicates that the situation has not improved since then, and may, in fact, have actually worsened.) Of the children under six covered by the survey, nearly half were cared for in their own homes. Home care may often be very good; in many cases, however, in the mother's absence, it is very poor.

WINDOWS ON DAY CARE

In 1971-72, I directed a study for the National Council of Jewish Women of day care needs and services in 77 cities. In the course of this project, which was published under the title "Windows on Day Care,"* hundreds of able women volunteers visited a large number of nonprofit and proprietary day care centers and family day care homes. They interviewed many mothers and talked with the many people in their communities most knowledgeable about day care. Interviews with working mothers underscored how difficult it was for many of them to arrange adequate home

*Windows on Day Care, a 1972 report based on findings of members of the National Council of Jewish Women, is available from the National Council office, 1 West 47th Street, New York, N.Y. 10036.

care for their children when they were on the job. Fewer than 4 percent of mothers have an adult female relative in the home who can assume care responsibility.

In a large percentage of the homes of working mothers, fathers work at night and expect to sleep during the day while trying to look after their children. In how many homes do fathers say to their children, "Wake me up when you're hungry"? Is this the developmental care a small child needs? In many families, Council survey participants found that siblings were kept home from school to take responsibility for children only a little younger than themselves. Few mothers who depend on maids or babysitters can afford to pay enough to obtain well-trained household helpers; few can afford "in-home" help at all. Therefore it is not surprising that so many mothers said they were unhappy with child care arrangements in their own homes.

According to the Women's Bureau/Children's Bureau survey, nearly one-third of the preschool children of working mothers were cared for in homes other than their own. Day care homes of relatives and neighbors, providing care for as many as two million children, are the largest single purveyor of day care for children outside their own homes. The great majority of these day care homes only provide custodial care. Only about five percent are licensed and hence subject to inspection. At their best, they are warm and loving; at their worst, they do serious harm.

Participants in the "Windows on Day Care" project visited a sizable number of day care homes. They reported that only six percent of those observed provided what was regarded as "superior" care. Twenty-nine percent were considered "good." Half were custodial in nature, providing little or no educational or other services beyond the meeting of physical needs. An additional fourteen percent were regarded as outright "poor"; all too many of these were shocking in the extreme. For example, an observer visited a day care home licensed for no more than six children. In this home there were 47 children cared for by one day care mother. Eight infants were tied to cribs; toddlers were tied to chairs; and three, four and five years olds coped as best they could.

Another observer reported:

> This interviewer can still recall vividly one particular home where she counted eleven children—five infants and six other small children from about one to four years old running and screaming in the four room house. The strong urine smell, the stale odor of un-eaten food everywhere, and the bugs crawling around made one nauseous. There was one very obese, sullen, unpleasant woman in charge.

Very little funding is available today for the badly needed training of day care mothers. Here is a report of an interview with still another day care mother who was not an isolated example: "We don't have toys," she said. She had had paper for coloring but "it got tore up." She said she "counted on the Lord to help her teach the right way with the help of a switch." Three year olds!

According to the Women's Bureau/Children's Bureau study study of the arrangements working mothers make for their children's care, fifteen percent of all children under six went with their mothers to their places of work. Experience in the early years has profound and irreversible effects. A large part of intelligence and behavior patterns is developed then. Will a child playing on the floor of a back room of a dry cleaning establishment have much opportunity to realize his or her potential?

There are two additional groups of children of working mothers to be accounted for. First and saddest of all are the "latchkey" kids, left on their own with no one to care for them. We don't know how many they are, but considerable numbers were reported in the cities included in the "Windows on Day Care" survey.

Here is a story, more telling than official statistics, which was included in the report of a Council survey participant:

> Peter, age three, gets his own lunch every day. He has to. No one else is home . . . He eats what he can reach and what his still uncoordinated hands can concoct if he can get the refrigerator or cabinet doors open. Some day it might be poison. Peter is anything but alone in his plight. The City Welfare Department estimates that 700 children less than six years of age are left alone each day, in our city alone, without any formal supervision when their mothers have to work.

There should not have to be any little children in America left alone to fend for themselves.

Finally, there are the children cared for in centers, both nonprofit and proprietary. The Women's Bureau/ Children's Bureau study found that only six percent of the preschool children of working mothers were cared for in these centers. The proportion of children in group care has risen since that study was made in 1965, but not very markedly.

Monitors for "Windows on Day Care" found that the great majority of the children cared for in the centers observed had working mothers. Proprietary centers primarily served middle- and higher-income families. The nonprofit centers largely enrolled children from very low income families, although some of them did accept a small proportion from middle-income families which were charged fees scaled to income.

Children from one-parent homes headed by working mothers were a small minority in most proprietary centers. The proprietary centers visited were generally too expensive for fatherless families. The nonprofit centers gave children from these families top priority. In two-thirds of the nonprofit centers visited by project participants, children from one-parent homes were a sizable majority.

About three-fourths of the day care centers observed were largely segregated institutions, serving only white or predominantly white families, or only black or predominantly black families.

FACTS ABOUT PROPRIETARY CENTERS

The average fee charged was about $18.50 a week per child. Survey participants felt that this was all that the great majority of families served could afford, yet they recognized that fees at this average level do not and cannot possibly buy developmental care including essential educational, nutritional, health and social services.

Because the average fee charged was less than half what quality care actually costs, parents got what they paid for. In more than half the proprietary centers the size of classes exceeded generally accepted standards, and the adult-child ratios were far too low.

Salaries paid center directors and other professional staff were, on the whole, very much lower than those paid elementary school personnel. The great majority received less than $4,000 a year, with many paid subminimum wage rates. Because salaries were so low, the majority of the staff had little or no training in early childhood education or development.

On the basis of the wide range of information collected, the proprietary centers visited were rated as providing "superior," "good," "fair" or "poor" care. Only one percent of the proprietary centers visited were considered "superior"; 14 percent were regarded as "good." An additional 36 percent were reported to be largely custodial, providing "fair" care in the sense of meeting basic physical needs, but with little, if any, developmental services. About half were considered to be rendering poor care; in some cases this was found to be actually injurious.

How poor can "poor" care be? A survey participant reported that at the time of her visit to a center there were two children, aged 10 and 12, in sole charge. Said the visitor:

> This center should be closed. Absolutely filthy. Toilets not flushed, and smelly. Broken equipment and doors. Broken windows on lower level near back stairs and doors. Broken chairs and tables. No indoor play equipment. One paper towel used to wipe the faces and hands of all children. Kitchen very, very dirty.

Another excerpt:

> Very poor, basement, dark room. All ages together. Rigid control and discipline. Rundown equipment. Babies are kept next door in double-decker cardboard cribs in a small room with a gas heater . . . a sad case of inhumane dehumanizing of kids by an owner who makes plenty of money.

NONPROFIT DAY CARE CENTERS

One the whole, the nonprofit centers presented a more encouraging picture. About 15 percent of the nonprofit centers visited were Head Start projects; about the same percentage were other programs wholly financed by public funds. About one quarter of all nonprofit centers visited were jointly financed by public and private funds, and another one quarter were centers run by philanthropic agencies. A few were hospital based. The remainder were largely church operated, generally run on a fee-for-service basis. On the whole, of all centers seen, the best of the Head Start centers elicited the most praise on the part of Council Survey participants.

While Head Start provided service without cost to parents, a large majority of the other nonprofit programs observed charged a flat fee, averaging about $14.00 a week. A few scaled their fees from nominal amounts upward, according to the income of parents.

Qualifications of directors of the nonprofit centers visited were much higher than those who headed centers under proprietary auspices, although there was relatively little difference in the degree of training of other staff members. Salaries paid were also far better in nonprofit than proprietary centers, both for professional personnel and aides. Costs of services generally run considerably higher in the former than the latter. To illustrate: in Washington, D.C. some 25 publicly financed centers are now run by the National Child Day Care Association and care for about 1200 children on a full-day basis. Costs per child average about $45 a week, whereas average fees in proprietary centers in the District are about half that amount. Although the Association's centers provide care of excellent quality, a recent survey made by a private research organization at the request of the city welfare authorities found the services of a large majority of the privately run centers to be far below acceptable minimum standards.

Adult-child ratios met generally accepted standards in a much higher proportion of the nonprofit than proprietary centers observed, and nonprofit centers were considerably more likely to provide the full range of services necessary for developmental care.

For these and other reasons, the services of the nonprofit centers observed were, on the whole, rated considerably higher than those of the proprietary centers visited.

Of all nonprofit centers seen, nearly ten percent were regarded by survey participants as "superior." Somewhat more than one quarter were considered "good," and about half were rated "fair," meaning that while they provided for basic physical needs they were essentially custodial. Somewhat more than ten percent were considered "poor."

The centers rated "superior" were heartwarming. They provided care as good as any to be found. Most of the "poor" centers seen should not be permitted to continue operating.

FUTURE NEEDS

Survey findings underscored the urgency of the need both to expand and greatly improve the quality of day care services for the children of working mothers. Many people have the impression that in the last few years the gap between need for care and its supply has been closing. Although supply has been rising, demand has been rising even faster.

In 1965, licensed day care homes and centers had the capacity to care for 25,000 children. By 1973, this enrollment capacity had risen to about 900,000 children. This gain, however, is not as encouraging as it looks. First, some of the increase in licensed capacity was more apparent than real. It simply reflected our growing efforts to license already existing homes and centers.

Secondly, during the eight years in which licensed enrollment capacity grew by 450,000, the number of children under the age of six of working mothers rose by nearly twice that number. We will have to run much faster just to stay in the same place.

Thirdly, most of the actual increase in enrollment was subsidized by public funding which came from Head Start, Title IV, WIN and Model City funds, among others. These programs made a vital contribution, but they have been largely restricted to the children of families in poverty. These are, of course, the children who should have the highest priority—but they represent a relatively small proportion of all children in need of care.

The number of working mothers who are not eligible for subsidized day care for their children but whose incomes are not sufficient to enable them to pay for good care is very large. About two thirds of all children whose mothers are in the labor force are in families with annual incomes between $5,000 and $15,000. Not many families in this income range can afford to pay for good full-day care which may cost from $2,000 to $3,000 or even more per child per year. The evidence indicates that, despite the recent increase in enrollment capacity, the day care crisis is intensifying.

Need is not only a matter of how many places there are, but also how adequate the places are, how accessible they are and how much they cost. Good infant care is extremely costly, much needed and almost nonexistent. Care at night and on weekends, when many mothers have to work, is almost impossible to come by.

The preschoolers of employed mothers are by no means the only little children who lack the developmental experiences good day care affords. A second group, no less in need, are those in economically and educationally disadvantaged poor or near-poor families in which the mothers are not employed. It is estimated that there are about two and one-half million of these children under the age of six, a large proportion of whom would benefit greatly from part-day programs providing educational, health, and other developmental opportunities. Head Start and similar programs, both publicly and philanthropically supported, reach only a very small proportion of these children.

In addition to children of working mothers, and children in economically disadvantaged homes in which the mother does not work, there are many others whose need for day care presents a compelling challenge. There are many handicapped children who can fare better outside their own homes, and children of mothers who are studying or in work training or whose volunteer services in the community make a vital contribution, and who would welcome good care for their children for part of the day. *All children whose parents desire it for them need good day care at an affordable price.*

The magnitude of unmet and inadequately met need is huge. Federal funds in far larger amounts must be appropriated. Where are we with respect to new federal legislation?

Federal Legislation

In 1971, Senator Walter Mondale (D.-Minn.) introduced a bill in the Senate calling for $2 billion for the next fiscal year for developmental child care programs—to plan, develop and operate "comprehensive physical and mental health, social and cognitive development services necessary for children participating in the programs."

A bill much like the Mondale bill, but differing in some respects, was introduced in the House by Representative John Brademas (D.-Ind.). Later the Mondale-Brademas measure was incorporated as a separate title in a bill to continue the nation's antipoverty programs. After long debate, the overall bill was passed by both houses of Congress and went to a conference committee to reconcile the differences in the Senate and House positions. After many weeks of discussion a compromise version was agreed to. This was approved in December, 1971 by a Senate vote of 63 to 17 and by a substantial House margin of 210 to 186.

The bill authorized $2 billion for the fiscal year starting July 1, 1972 for comprehensive child development services. Of this, $500 million was for the continuation of Head Start programs. These programs, without question, would have widened the horizons of thousands of disadvantaged children.

Special set-asides were provided, with 100 percent federal funding, for programs for migrant, Indian and handicapped children. Other direct service programs were to receive 80 percent federal funding. The 20 percent nonfederal share was to be provided through public or private funds in the form of cash, services and other contributions in kind.

In addition to supporting comprehensive services, as much as 15 percent of the funds were to be available for loans and grants for construction of facilities. This would have been a much-welcomed addition, for there has been little help for construction up to now and the shortage of facilities has been a serious bottleneck. In addition, money was to be available for renting and remodeling facilities, for training personnel, for research to improve early childhood education techniques, for model programs and, of course, for administration at the federal, state and local levels.

Major action was called for at the local level. Every locality with a population of more than 5,000, or cooperating groups of localities wishing to participate, were to set up two bodies. The first was the prime sponsoring local administrative agency to be responsible for contracting projects with a wide range of public and private nonprofit agencies and organizations. Each program in the prime sponsorship area was to include plans for surveys of needs, and for the development of comprehensive services to children from a wide range of socioeconomic backgrounds. Active parent participation was called for. Above all, programs and services were to be provided only for children whose parents requested them.

The second local body was to be the Child Development Council responsible for planning, supervising, coordinating, monitoring and evaluating the programs. It was to approve the goals, policies, actions and procedures of the prime sponsor. At least half the members of the Council were to be parents of children served in the programs. The other members were to be appointed by the mayor or appropriate governing body to represent the various public and voluntary groups concerned.

Comprehensive services were to be available without charge to families of four with incomes under $4,320. Families with incomes above this level up to $6,600 were to pay $280 a year and families with incomes between $6,600 and $6,950 were to pay a small additional amount. The Secretary of HEW would have set fees according to income for children of families with incomes exceeding $6,950. These income eligibility figures would have varied with the size of the family and with some reference to the cost of living in the locality.

The $2 billion proposed outlay was small relative to need and to our capacity to invest in the future of our children. It represented less than one fifth of one percent of the value of the then total national output. Closing one major tax loophole could give us far more than $2 billion. A very small cutback in military outlays would more than cover costs. What are our children worth? In 1970, our nation spent more than five times this amount on tobacco alone, and more than eight times as much for alcoholic beverages.

The bill, which would have enabled us to make an excellent step forward, was warmly supported by hundreds of public interest groups, organizations of educators, of women, and of labor, by church groups, social welfare agencies and many others.

Nevertheless, it was vetoed by former President Nixon, who said, on December 9, 1971, "neither the immediate need nor the desirability of a national child development program of this character has been demonstrated." He felt the proposed outlays were excessive. He considered the bill "the most radical piece of legislation to emerge from the Ninety-second Congress" and to have "family weakening implications."

Many thousands of letters had reached the White House, it is reported, in opposition to the bill. They were largely inspired, we are told, by a single organization which has never been concerned with child welfare and which has long opposed even the most moderate social welfare advances as dangerous and unaffordable. Very few supporting groups communicated with the White House—a very sad failure of the democratic process.

The struggle for urgently needed progress had to begin all over again. In the spring of 1972, Senator Mondale again introduced a Child Development measure, and a compromise was reached with a similar bill sponsored by Senator Jacob Javits (R-N.Y.) and overwhelming bipartisan support was rallied. A vote of 73 in favor, versus 12 against, was registered.

The S.3617 bill, as passed, differed in some major respects from the legislation approved in 1971. The funds authorized were sharply cut. For fiscal year 1973 only $150 million was approved for training and planning, with $1.2 billion for fiscal 1974 for program operations and $1.6 billion for fiscal 1975.

The federal share of cost of programs was set at 90 percent. The 10 percent local share could be in cash or in kind. The bill gave priority to continue funding of Head Start projects, authorizing $500 million of program funds for these and other programs serving low-income children. It should be noted that profit-making programs were not excluded from eligibility for public funds.

A locality would have needed at least 25,000 people to be eligible for prime sponsorship. However, an amendment from the floor (introduced by Senator Dominick) permitted the Secretary of HEW to make the choice when more than one sponsor applied to serve an area. This would have placed state and local governments in competition for prime sponsorship. The administration would thus have had the means, if it so chose to opt for state control. Under the bill, five states were enabled to set up demonstration state-controlled plans, with no local prime sponsors allowed.

The bill as approved by the Senate required 50 percent parent membership on the National Child and Family Services Council and Local Program Councils, which were to approve the plans and policies of the prime sponsors, and 50 percent parent membership on Project Policy Committees of each operating program.

After a long delay in action in the House, Congressman Ogden Reid—who had left the Republican Party to join the Democratic ranks, citing the President's December 1971 veto of the Child Development Bill as his reason for doing so—introduced a companion bill, which did not emerge from committee.

Day care forces were so vigorously involved throughout 1973 in opposing changes in Social Service Regulations proposed by the Department of Health, Education and Welfare, which would have deprived many children of publicly funded day care services had they been promulgated, that legislative action with respect to expanded federally supported day care programs came to a standstill.

In 1974 constructive measures were again in the legislative hopper. Senators Mondale and Javits, with the cosponsorship of 22 additional Senators, again introduced a bill, "The Child and Family Services Act of 1974" (S.3754). On the House side, Congressman Brademas, with more than 60 co-sponsors, introduced a companion proposal (H.R.15882) which differs in some respects from the Senate measure.

The bills are designed to provide financial assistance to help the states and localities improve and expand services for children and families. They adhere to the main principles contained in the proposals which passed the Congress in 1971, and which were accepted by the Senate in 1972.

During the first year of the bills, if enacted, $150 million would be authorized for planning, training and technical assistance. In the second year $200 million would be authorized for continued planning and preparation, with $500 million available for upgrading programs. For the third and final year, there is a $1 billion authorization for improving and expanding services and programs.

The bills would provide free day care for children in families with incomes below the lower living standard budget of the U.S. Department of Labor (now $8,118 for an urban family of four and varying according to family size). A sliding fee schedule would begin at that point to permit families with incomes above that level to receive day care services at fees scaled to income so that they could afford them. Sixty-five percent of the funds would be reserved for serving children from families with incomes up to the lower living standard budget, with up to 35 percent of the funds available to serve children in higher income families, with priority to children of working mothers and single parents.

The bills are designed to assure that any services funded are quality services. Standards would have to be consistent with the 1968 Federal Interagency Day Care Requirements, and funds for monitoring and enforcing them are specifically provided.

Like the earlier measures, the bills are designed to maximize parent participation and control and strengthen family life. The wide variety of programs which would be funded would be entirely voluntary and would be administered through a system of state and local governmental "prime sponsors." Unlike the bills introduced in 1971 and 1972, no minimum population requirement has been set for localities to qualify as "prime sponsors."

Senator Mondale, in introducing S.3754 said:

> I want to emphasize at this point that we do not have the final answer to the question of what delivery system is best. Our goal is to explore this question very deeply throughout the hearings and investigations of this bill. We want to develop a system that will insure parental involvement to assure coordination and maximum use of resources available. We intend to invite testimony and views from representatives from Federal, State and local governments, child and family service specialists, as well as other experts as we seek to discover the best allocation of administrative responsibility among the various levels of government . . .
>
> This bill is designed to provide the substance necessary to achieve the national commitment called for five years ago. It is our best thinking after five years

of legislative investigation, and passage of several previous bills, about the way to best provide for the wide variety of programs, and services that families need. But nothing in this bill is etched in stone.

We want the advice and counsel of families, and of a wide variety of individuals and organizations experienced and knowledgeable about child care and child services from all sections of the country as we begin hearings and investigations on this bill. I believe I speak for all the sponsors of this legislation, when I say that we are open, indeed anxious, to receive suggestions and recommendations about ways to strengthen and improve this bill.

Thus the bills' proponents have opened the door wide to constructive input on the part of those concerned with meeting the nation's day care needs. Action on the bills is unlikely in 1974. But with the strong support of the advocates of children, strong, sound legislation can be enacted early in 1975 by so large a majority in both Houses of Congress that the possibility of a presidential veto would be highly unlikely. We cannot, as a country, continue to ignore one of our most urgent items of unfinished business on the social action agenda. What people need, want and support does have a way of eventually occurring in this great democracy of ours.

STATE AND LOCAL ACTION NEEDED

The states and localities cannot afford to wait for federal legislation, however, before they rise to the many challenges. They have vital jobs to do. They need to review and update state and local day care standards which are antiquated in too many areas.

States and localities must increase their appropriations to fulfill their responsibility to enforce standards. Many states set standards but impose little or no penalty for violation. One large state has never revoked a license. How many states have been able to bring more than a small fraction of all the day care homes within their licensing orbit?

FUTURE ACTION

Are we reshaping enforcement so that it is more than merely a policing mechanism? It should become a consultative service that can help day care mothers and private and public centers to upgrade the quality of their facilities.

Can we help bring groups of day care mothers into some formal or informal relationship with first-rate day care centers? They could learn from each other, exchange personnel, arrange for an interchange of children, borrow equipment, have the use of a common library and share services they couldn't otherwise afford.

Are we doing all we can locally to mobilize our universities, our community colleges and our other educational institutions to provide training courses and workshops to improve the skills of day care personnel?

Educators could play a much larger role if they were called on more fully. We are still in the early stages of development of curriculum and educational techniques. The day care explosion that lies ahead will not only require many newly trained professionals; it will call for even larger numbers of paraprofessionals and the building of career ladders for them.

Should not our secondary schools do more toward developing courses on family life and child development for boys as well as girls? Voluntary field work in day care centers and after-school programs could be an important part of these programs—good for teenagers, good for children and good for the families of the future.

The immense unmet need for before-and-after-school care is numerically an even larger problem. Here we have hardly moved as a nation, although a few communities are constructively moving ahead. Are we using our schools as we should to provide this service? They are in the neighborhoods where the children are. The plant and equipment are available and the major overhead costs are already met. It is not so much money as concern, gumption and vigorous leadership that is needed to put these programs on the road.

Another challenge to our communities is the mounting of education programs to help parents understand what the components of developmental child care actually are. Many parents are complacent about the very poor care their children now receive because they do not always know the difference between good and bad care and how to choose between the alternatives. An educational and involvement program to reach them is imperative. Federal legislation alone, no matter how constructive, cannot begin to provide all the answers.

We must go forward together if we are to serve our children well. Even if S.3754-H.R.15882, the Mondale-Brademas bills now before Congress, were to become law, this legislation would not automatically provide needed coordination of new programs with those now in existence. Effective coordination of day care efforts at every level—especially at the local level—has become more important than ever before.

There is much to do. But it is all "do-able"! And do it we must. What splendid opportunities we have—if only we rise to them—to help every child realize his or her potentials and fulfill the aspirations all parents have for their children

Chapter Two

DAY CARE:
ISSUES, TRENDS AND DIRECTIONS

Therese W. Lansburgh

Society has traditionally approached the needs of its children from a deficit model; that is, as signs of abnormal behavior manifested themselves, treatment has been initiated when available. We now know that many problems can be avoided by early attention. As the Joint Commission on Mental Health of Children reported, "Our lack of commitment is a national tragedy. We know already that it is more fruitful to prevent damage to our young children than to attempt to patch and heal the wounds. We know that much of the damage can be avoided in the first three years of life. We know that the basis for mental development and competence is established largely by the age of six" (p.7). Society long has accepted the necessity of assisting in and sometimes even assuming total child rearing responsibilities in time of crisis. Now society is beginning to recognize the necessity for providing preventive and support services to supplement the family during the child's dependent years, rather than waiting to repair damages that might have been avoided. Day care services can provide the most effective program for preventing developmental deficiencies in young children.

Changing patterns in our society bear directly on child rearing practices, and hence, on the issues, trends and directions in child care. Our society is becoming increasingly industrialized, urbanized and peer-oriented, and more women, especially mothers, are going to work. Today's mobile and usually isolated family is responsible for meeting more of the needs of its members than the extended family of earlier days, but it has fewer resources to call upon in emergencies or for ongoing support. Young parents, increasingly the products themselves of nuclear rather than extended families, have lacked the opportunity to relate to a wide base of relatives and other adult models. They belong instead to a peer-oriented society which frequently does not offer sufficient experience in child rearing techniques with children of all ages. In crowded cities the lack of space in apartments compounds the lack of recreational areas outdoors. Television preempts a large portion of the working day, reducing interpersonal communication, physical activity, creative play and the joy of learning by doing. Single-parent families and superficial contacts within the community deprive many young children of role models, of the opportunity to develop problem-solving and decision-making competence and to deal with emotions.

In these situations, lacking the resources of family and long-established friends, the overworked and isolated parents must depend almost entirely on their own initiatives, often severely limiting the social and educational opportunities of their children. Thus the paradox is created whereby research increasingly emphasizes the importance of infant and childhood development, while parents are less and less able to provide the attention their children need.

Within the past ten years, research in child development in the medical, psychiatric, psychological, educational and related fields has underscored the importance of early experiences in determining later behavior, learning and problem-solving ability, innovation, social competence and physical and emotional health.

For the purposes of our discussion the most important findings of researchers are:

That the period of infancy and childhood lays the foundation for the growth and development of the human organism. The perception that actions can affect the environment, which replaces a sense of helplessness and impotence, is formed in these early years;

That the establishment of a sense of trust in another person, usually, although not necessarily, the biological mother, is the basis for all other development and exploration. Continuity, consistency and loving care, nurtured together by the family and day care program, provide the security and self-esteem necessary for continuing developmental progress;

That all aspects of development, e.g., physical and mental health and personality and character development, are interrelated. A malnourished or otherwise physically or emotionally disadvantaged child is preoccupied with inner struggles relating to basic needs for love, security and stability which distract him from the learning process. Maladjustment affecting cognitive development, attainment of the child's full potential and problem-solving ability inevitably results from deprivation in his early years;

That the developmental tasks of infancy and childhood can be encouraged or retarded by experimental opportunity. For example, communicative skills are largely developed by the age of three, and are largely dependent on the amount and type of vocalization to which the child is exposed during those years;

That the growth of organ functions occurs at certain critical periods. These functions do not develop fully if proper conditions do not exist at the right time. The brain grows faster during gestation and the first eighteen months of life than it ever does again. Malnutrition at this time as well as at later periods, can affect attention span, energy, and other components of cognition. Malnutrition at this crucial time can result in irreversible damage to the developing basic mental machinery (Lourie, 1971, pp. 33-39);

That, similarly, the development of aspects of personality and intelligence of patterns, and, for mastering and coping, occur at specific, optimal periods. Although developmental lags to some extent, can be made up later, evidence shows that one's original potential never can be attained once the period for optimal development has passed. The human organism does not proceed properly to the next stage unless it has integrated the previous stages satisfactorily;

That environment determines the development of an individual's coping and cognitive abilities to a much greater degree than was previously suspected. The President's Commission on Mental Retardation in 1963 underscored the extent of interacting between hereditary potentials and environmental factors by reporting that only 25 percent of the nation's retardates are genetically retarded. The other 75 percent, the Commission found, were retarded as a result of sociocultural factors, such as lack of adequate nutrition and lack of developmental opportunities, and not because of their inborn potential;

That early diagnosis of vulnerable children and treatment with positive programs to structure and improve environmental variables is possible and constructively preventing or ameliorating handicapping conditions (President's Committee on Mental Retardation, 1968);

That cognitive behavior evolves from personal experiences with the physical world to the social and finally to the ideational world (Maier, 1965);

That development is a cumulative process, with the growth of a sense of trust, a positive self-concept, of patterns of competence and problem-solving building in a sequential order on the innate genetic potential. Early deficits therefore can affect later growth adversely, but early intervention, conversely, can have delayed as well as immediate beneficial results as new stages of growth build on early foundations.*

This points out the need for programs starting as early as junior high school to educate parents and prospective parents in child growth and development and child rearing practices, and for comprehensive day care programs; which are also a logical first step in delivering preventive, rather than deficit-oriented, resources for children.

Translating these broad developmental imperatives into programs to foster optimal human development presents a challenge involving the full range of social service professionals. Their combined efforts not only can deliver the preventive programs children need, but perhaps more importantly, can reeducate parents and the general public so as to dispel the negative attitudes toward child care that have impeded the expansion of day care services. For too long the idea of day care has suffered because the public

*The key word here is "cumulative." The expectation that programs of intervention that could make a startling impact on accumulated deficits would continue to maintain that impact over additional years without follow-up or other changes in life patterns was unrealistic. Having expected too much initially from a program of limited duration, many are saying that programs do not "work." Many compensatory programs do prove extremely beneficial to children. However, a supportive continuum is necessary if gains established in quality preschool and day care programs are to be mtaintained in the school years. Many scholars believe that approximately 80 percent of intelligence is inherited, and only 20 percent is affected by environmental factors. There are others who believe that intelligence is much more susceptible to environmental influence. However, even if research were to prove the hypothesis of "only" 20 percent, a 20 percent difference in intellectual ability is a considerable factor in individual lives and could mean the difference between marginal functioning and the ability to perform within the normal range. A technological society has less call for unskilled labor, and it becomes increasingly important that citizens perform at capacity.

has associated it almost exclusively with deprived children and inadequate parents. Day care has been seen only in terms of a custodial "care and protection" approach, rather than as a developmental opportunity. Public policymakers, by incorporating child care services into public assistance programs under the administrative control of the agencies responsible for the poor, dependent and deviant, have caused many middle class parents to fail to see that these services are a resource for their own children, deserving of their interest and support.

Day care services and programs have taken many forms, including nursery school, kindergarten, child development centers, Head Start, family day care and babysitting situations. The day care programs of greatest usefulness and quality should provide developmental child care wherein the child is learning, exploring, creating, integrating and organizing his experiences. The *Encyclopedia of the National Association of Social Workers* states that a quality service should provide: (1) a strong educational program geared to the age, ability, interests and temperamental organization of each child; (2) adequate nutrition; (3) a health program, and health services when needed; (4) an opportunity for social and emotional growth through a balance between group experiences and opportunities for solitude and internalization of ideas and experiences; (5) opportunities for parent education, participation and involvement; and (6) social services as needed by the child and his family (Lansburgh, 1970, p. 116).

The Developmental Child Care Forum of the 1970 White House Conference on Children called for a comprehensive network of child care services for all children who need it and all families who seek it. First priority at 100 percent funding should be provided for children of families in greatest need, with a sliding scale for families above the poverty level.

Considerable resistance to child care exists among

those who see it as a threat to the traditional family structure. Undoubtedly the family remains humankind's most enduring social institution. It has not endured without change; the source of its durability has been its very ability to adapt and evolve to meet varying internal and external pressures brought about by changes in the physical and social environment. Most of those who argue against the establishment of a system of day care on the grounds that it will foster the break-up of the home ignore many changes that have already taken place. Society long ago recognized the wisdom of delegating certain of its child rearing responsibilities, most notably education, to trained professionals. In addition, millions of mothers, forced by economic necessity, have already left their homes for full- and part-time employment. Many mothers contribute to the economic progress of this country, as well as to that of their own families, through participation in the work force. According to the U.S. Census Bureau, over one half of the female population is working, including over one third of mothers. More mothers of young children are going to work before the child enters school.† Recent research shows the cognitive and socializing advantages of developmental, supportive environments for young children, advantages which have long been recognized in part-day programs such as kindergartens and nursery schools for the children of mothers who are at home, and are even more important for children whose mothers are at work for a large portion of the day. Evidence exists that children do not tend to suffer maternal deprivation effects when they are returned to their mothers, even if they spend a large part of their waking hours away from their mothers—provided there is not a deficit of mothering during the hours mother and child are together, and provided that developmental opportunities and experiences, securi-

†*Monthly Labor Review*, U.S. Department of Labor, based on March 1973 survey.

ty, stability, warmth and nurture of a sense of self confidence are fostered in his day care experiences.

Rather than promote a radical restructuring of society, advocates of child care ask merely that society keep pace with changes in family organization by providing services for children who might otherwise suffer from neglect, and for parents who might otherwise suffer from economic deprivation or the frustrations of unfulfilled personal ambition. We cannot allow the sociological lag between fact and fantasy to continue. To establish a system of day care services is to recognize that society has the responsibility and the opportunity to supplement the family and assist it when necessary to meet its child rearing responsibilities.

One obstacle to extensive day care program funding has been its demonstrated relatively high cost per child; a cost that usually is greater than public school programs. For example Head Start annual expenditures averaged $2000 per child. The reasons are fairly obvious. The hours are longer, the program runs year-round rather than for just nine months, and the staff-child ratio must be higher for younger children, as is the case, of course, in any program incorporating individual attention and supplementary services. Anything less in a day care program would not serve the developmental needs of children. No progress would be made for the child's benefit and any expenditures would be wasted.

Resistance to day care comes also from those who cite the traditions of child care in totalitarian countries in which social and political indoctrination is a stated objective. These countries, whether in Germany or the Soviet Union or China, contend that the primary responsibility for child rearing lies with the state and provide training that often conflicts directly with the traditional values and culture of parents.

In the United States, in contrast, child care programs almost without exception have stressed the necessity of parental participation at every level of their activities. Most day care programs make a concerted effort to incorporate, at least in theory, the values and standards of the families they serve, and emphasize the need for open communication between the parents and the staff of the program. The focus here is on society's final responsibility in fostering child growth and development when parents need help in fulfilling their child rearing responsibilities.

The special Task Force on the Delivery of Services of the Developmental Child Care Forum of the 1970 White House Conference on Children deliberated on many issues concerning the extent and nature of parental participation in child care programs. Following the establishment of rigorous but flexible national standards and goals regarding facilities, staffing and program elements, parental control of local programs was deemed crucial. Aware that the issue of parental control has generated conflicts in many communities, the Task Force nonetheless asserted that whatever frictions may result, cooperation and a feeling of equal partnership between parents and child care staff is central to the health of the programs. The Task Force recommended that at least one half of the places on the boards of operating centers should be filled by parents and that the ultimate power to hire and fire, at least in the case of the director, should rest with the parents of enrolled children. Parental involvement and ultimate control of day care programs maintains parental involvement with their children and ensures that the programs supplement, rather than substitute for, the family. Parental involvement can facilitate a flow of information on child growth and development from child care professionals to the parents, and can also provide child care workers with the data necessary to tailor their programs to the families they serve. This flow of information can foster better child rearing as parents gain greater confidence in themselves and their ability to influence their own and their children's destiny.

Undertaking a national commitment to child care services raises many complex issues and requires an enormous political and administrative effort. Current research outlines the broad parameters for the future, but does not delineate in programmatic terms what policy or program concept should be implemented. Given the realities of today's society, how can we design and implement a new service delivery system, building on knowledge of delivery systems in other areas, and yet utilizing to the fullest the advantages that a comparatively clean slate offers us? How do we combat inertia and the effort to retain the status quo by maintaining existing but inadequate approaches and positions? How do we keep the focus on children and present day care from becoming a battleground for other forces and other issues?

In the complicated process of establishing what is essentially a massive new delivery system for human services with a preventive rather than a deficit orientation, we must recognize that some mistakes will be unavoidable. However, gains will greatly outweigh mistakes if a properly structured and adequately funded quality program is established.

A basic issue is the question of auspices. Which agency will have the responsibility for mounting and directing this massive new program? Health, education and welfare all have contributions to make to day care services. Health is a vital part of the growth of all children—but in only a few states is the Department of Health involved in day care; in these instances it is responsible for licensing, but the Department of Welfare (or Social Services or Human Resources) maintains control of the purse strings. Similarly, the Department of Education is the operational agency only in a handful of states. Many feel that education, regarded as the biggest business in the country, has enough to do setting its own house in order without attempting to establish a new system of preschool services. Others are concerned that educators who are wedded to the strictly structured curriculum of older children will apply rote learning and sitting still as standards also applicable to younger children, whose special need is to learn by doing with maximal freedom of movement.

The various potential and current auspices of day care programs constitute a central issue for greater consideration and decision. The decisions made will have an impact on the quality of care, its level, organization and acceptibility to parents. Health, education and welfare all have contributions to make to day care services. Governmental funding, of course, will result in government control. Only government—federal, state and local—will have the financial resources necessary for basic financing of day care on the scale contemplated, although the private, proprietary, business and voluntary sectors can make substantial, and even vital, contributions. However, placing day care within the jurisdiction of state or local welfare systems may well limit its fullest acceptability, effectiveness and utilization. An eventual transition to a more broadly based administrative focus becomes very difficult when the original base of operations is welfare oriented. Such a situation occurred when New York State put its Medicaid program under the Welfare Department, rather than under the Health Department, thus shifting the major focus from delivery of good quality health services to an emphasis on eligibility determination. In order to avoid this, the Conference Forum recommended that at the national level the Office of Child Development administer the day care program. At the state and local level, the OCD could sidestep the stigma which today is attached to programs placed within the welfare system. If it is our goal to enrich and enlarge the child's experiential base and to supplement the family in its child rearing responsibilities, then we are talking about a service which ultimately will be considered a social utility, comparable to today's public schools, for rich and poor, with no eligibility requirements attached.

Many programs and sources of funds dealing with various aspects of child care already exist in the federal government and in state and local governments. Thus, initial efforts in the field of child care will involve not starting from scratch, but sorting through, weeding out and combining existing programs. The need, then, is for a free flow of information, widespread cooperation and coordination to evolve a whole new administrative structure. The existing duplication of effort and the lack of coordination of current programs render even less effective than they need to be the present-day, meager levels of funding.

In order to secure the massive funding necessary for a nationwide commitment to child care, an enormous effort will be required to inform the public of the need for it. Several organizations exist to contribute to this effort, among them the Day Care and Child Development Council of America. Such organizations are catalysts working to encourage the groundswell of interest and concern about children and day care on the part of a broad spectrum of professionals, parents, volunteers and citizens in all walks of life. Local efforts are encouraged to expand services and to coordinate their efforts in a national thrust. The Council circulates news in the field through its own publications and promotes a public education effort that is vital in order to create the attitudes that will demand and support developmental services in this country.

The Child Welfare League of America is another organization devoted to improving and continuing vital standard-setting and program concerns, as well as its publications which are primarily for professionals.

Children cannot speak for themselves. Government employees are limited in their right to speak on legislative issues. Tax-exempt organizations are allowed to devote no more than five percent of their total activities to legislation and funding, even though these issues are crucial in determining the options of many youngsters. Every other interest group has joined together to represent its case on the issues that are of concern to it. Children deserve the protection that adequate representation of their needs and interests would foster. Only through an organization that is not tax-exempt and which is broadly representative of citizens of all walks of life and professionals of many disciplines, will children secure the care, protection and developmental opportunities which should be their birthright.

By recognizing early the sources of later deficiency and dysfunction in our young children, and by making concerted efforts through developmental day care programs, we can make great strides toward enabling every person to reach his fullest social and intellectual potential. Much of the tragedy of wasted lives, not to mention the enormous expense of institutionalization and remedial programs, could be prevented by applying the vast expertise and professional resources of this country to the fundamentals of healthy growth.

Conclusion

The Parents and Children Forum of the White House Conference stated that,

> America's children and their families are in trouble, trouble so deep and pervasive as to threaten the future of our nation. The source of the trouble is nothing less than a national neglect of children . . . Our national rhetoric notwithstanding, the actual patterns of life in America today are such that children and families come last. . . . The failure to reorder our priorities, the insistence on business as usual and the continued reliance on rhetoric as a substitute for fundamental reforms can only have one result: the far more rapid and pervasive growth of alienation, apathy, drugs, delinquency and violence among the young and not so young, in all segments of our national life. Surely this is a road to national destruction. This is not the road for America.

Our society still has the capacity and the value commitment necessary to reverse the trend.

The challenge is great—to create a national commitment to fulfill the needs of children and families; to meet part of that need through a system of developmental day care services; and, setting aside personal considerations, to deliver that system in a manner that will promote the optimal development of America's chidren. If we can base our actions on our new knowledge of child growth and development and apply it to our children, we will have before us the possibility of a Human Revolution that will do for today's society what the Industrial Revolution did for the society of its day.

REFERENCES

Erikson, E. H. *Childhood and society.* N.Y.: W.W. Norton, 1950. (2nd ed., 1963).

Joint Commission on Mental Health of Children. *Crisis in child mental health: challenge for the 1970's* N.Y.: Harper and Row, 1969.

Lansburgh, T. Child welfare: day care of children. *Encyclopedia of Social Work,* 1970, **I**, (16).

Lourie, R. The first three years of life: an overview of a new frontier in psychiatry. *The American Journal of Psychiatry,* May 1971, **127**(11).

Maier, H. W. *Three theories of child development. The contributions of Erik Erikson, Jean Piaget and Robert R. Sears and their applications.* N.Y.: Harper and Row, 1965.

The President's Committee on Mental Retardation. Washington, D.C.: U.S. Government Printing Office, 1968.

Proceedings of the 1970 White House Conference on Children. Washington, D.C.: Developmental Child Care Forum, 1970.

Chapter Three

HISTORICAL PRECEDENTS FOR DAY CARE

Dorothy Hewes

Present-day controversies over the most valuable methods of child care can perhaps best be viewed against the backdrop of history. Just as figure-ground perception is important in reading readiness, so is the clarity of today's problems brought out when seen against the tapestry of years gone by.

We tend to view the past, if we try to visualize it at all, as a cozy cottage scene with mother stirring a pot of porridge at the hearth while rosy children tumble about. Stark facts contradict this image. Perhaps the problems of how to care for children, and who should care for them, are as old as the human race; certainly some of the higher mammals have well-organized systems for the use of mother substitutes.

Earliest records (Trexler, 1973, pp. 99-100) of child care institutions indicate that they were set up as an alternative to infanticide. The first foundling home seems to have been established in Milan in 787 in order to save children from death, and five hundred years later Pope Innocent III founded the hospital of the Santo Spirito in Rome because so many women were throwing their children into the Tiber. In 1294, the asylum of San Gallo was established in

Florence to prevent crimes against infants and to sustain the poor, and the new foundling institution of the Innocenti a century and a half later was also maintained so that innocents would not have to suffer a brutal death and be condemned to an eternity without baptism and without God. Trexler reports that infant murders, attributed in some cases to suffocation or to witches, persisted until modern times.

In medieval society, not only was there little concern for institutional care of children, but there was also little awareness of the fact of "childhood" as such. Infants too young to contribute labor to the household were just not counted; those who survived to a useful age were considered small people and expected to perform accordingly. Ariés (1962) has pointed out that by the fourteenth century families were beginning to pay attention to the amusing antics of their offspring, and that by the seventeenth century, moralists were writing tracts critical of coddling. By the end of that century parents were beginning to think of children as fragile creatures of God, and by the eighteenth, they were expressing concern for their children's health and hygiene, (Ariés, 1962, p. 133). Although families were starting to value their children, the nuclear family as we know it did not live in privacy. Before the eighteenth century, the homes of prosperous Europeans were also places of business, with swarms of servants, relatives, apprentices and friends sharing the beds and meals. Even into the nineteenth century, the largest and poorest segment of the population did not have homes as we visualize them; we forget that this is an aristocratic concept.

During these years, an aspect of child life that is often ignored, but that was certainly related to child care, was the custom of sending newborn infants out into villages to avoid the pestilence of the city. Ariés claims that there were no babies in Paris during the seventeenth century. The practice had started long before, and it continued in upper and middle class households until the late 1800's; around that time, wet nurses were gradually moved into the city homes, so that children lived with their parents once again. Only poor children were given cow's milk or its substitutes (Ariés, 1962, p. 374). Although physicians and philanthropists campaigned for establishing maternal colonies near the cities to provide both wetnurses and cow's milk adoption of this practice was slow (Ariés, 1962, pp. 374-375).

During these years, also, we must remember that one war after another led to devastation of the countryside and disruption of normal life. Hygienic practices were virtually nonexistent and the death rate among small children was high. Certainly, there was no need and no demand for any institution resembling our modern day nurseries.

The first known institution to combine child care with an educational purpose seems to have been started in 1769 by John Frederic Oberlin, a pastor assigned to the village of Waldbach in northeastern France. Like much of Europe, this district had been decimated by the Thirty Years War. There were no roads, no tools, no knowledge of anything but the most primitive farming. Oberlin's predecessor as pastor recounted to him his conversation with the local schoolmaster, described as a withered old man who lay on a little bed in one corner of the room in which some vile and noisy children were collected.

"What do you teach the children?"
"Nothing, sir."
"Nothing? How is that?"
"Because I know nothing myself."
"Why, then, are you instituted schoolmaster?"
"Why, sir, I had been taking care of the Waldbach pigs for a great number of years, and when I got too old and infirm for that employment, they sent me here to take care of the children" (Gosden, 1969, p. 46).

Within a few years, there was evidence of prosperity. Oberlin formed schools and supported "conductrices" for each community. Children of two and three were taught to sit for periods of instruction, while those of five and six, boys and girls alike, were given lessons in knitting, spinning and sewing. Illustrations of colored Scriptures or natural history were used, and place names were taught using local maps engraved on wood. While the children were in school parents were engaged in community activities and employment.

As the age of hand labor, of home-based industry, evolved with the Industrial Revolution into the factory system, working women in the European cities faced child care problems similar to ours today. One alternative was the dame school. These schools were often kept by elderly and impoverished women, such as the one described by William Shenstone:

> In every little village marked with little spire,
> Embowered in trees and hardly known to fame,
> There dwells in lowly shed and mean attire,
> A matron old, whom we Schoolmistress name,
> Who boasts unruly brats with birch to tame.

Another school, described in the Report of the Committee on the Council on Education in 1840, enrolled 31 children, from two to seven years of age. It was in a cellar ten feet square by seven feet high. There was one window, 18 inches square, not made to open. Although it was August, the door was closed and a fire was burning. The dame explained that if there was no fire, the walls dripped with moisture. To keep children from falling into the fire, she had pushed them into the area by her bed. The door was closed to keep them from rushing out. Six children had brought tattered books; the only other teaching aids were a jar of candy and a cane. The dame paid her rent by being "Schoolmistress," but she bewailed her fate (Gosden, 1969, pp. 8-9).

Some dame schools were run by educated women who needed the income; some were part-day programs designed to teach beginning reading. At best, they were a reasonable solution for the working mother whose hours were long and whose pay was minimal.

A second alternative was child labor. Children of the poor were often sold as apprentices, which meant virtual slavery. Knox reported that ". . . between Spitalfields and Bethnal Green . . . a market for the hire of children is held on Mondays and Tuesdays between 6 and 7 A.M. . . . A father or mother brings her child to the market! They cry them like common merchandise . . . they deliver them . . . to the dissolute as readily as to the master of regular habits" (Vicinus, 1972, p. 80).

Although child labor laws were enacted, inspection was lax and enforcement negligible. In England, despite an 1819 Act excluding children under nine from employment in the mills, many were at work by five. One child was found at work before he had reached his second birthday. A certain Sir James Graham prophesied the ruin of British industry and the fall of the nation if legislation were enacted to reform such conditions.

In the mines, similar conditions existed. The youngest children were assigned the easy job of "trapper," with the duty of opening doors in the tunnels to let horses and workers pass and then quickly closing them for safety. Older children pushed carriages of coal when the tunnels were too small for horses; sexual equality was observed, for naked boys and girls worked together in the dark steaminess of the tunnels. One great mine owner, the Marquis of Londonderry, protested the threat of regulations which would limit this work to boys over ten, since the equilibrium of society would be destroyed If children were not at work until such an advanced age as that, how were parents to bring them up? Such a rule was not successful in England until 1860, but child labor was at last almost abolished by the early 1900's according to Salmon (1904).

If children were not in a dame school or at work, what was to be done? One further alternative was the innovation which became known in England as the "infant school." Even that term is controversial, the focus of one of the classic rivalries in child care history. Samuel Wilderspin testified that his 1820 establishment in London was the first authentic infant school, and that others were merely collections of young children. In any case, because Wilderspin spent much time during the next thirty years in lecturing throughout England, he left his mark on the development of early childhood education.

The original idea of the infant school is attributed to Robert Owen, a wealthy cotton mill owner who had attended school only between the ages of five and nine. He left school to work in a little country shop, moved to a position as apprentice to a draper and formed the Chorleton Twist Company when he was 23. After his marriage to the daughter of a mill owner in Scotland, he began a series of social and industrial experiments which extended over the next quarter century. His father-in-law considered himself an unusually humane employer, since he housed his imported child labor in decent dormitories and gave them good food to eat. The children worked from 6 A.M. to 7 P.M.; many children ran away and others were deformed physically. Owen built housing for families and established schooling for children between the ages of two and ten. His "New Institute" opened in 1816, a large building with a yard for children under six. Owen hired James Buchanan, whom he considered to have simplicity of mind and a kind heart, and a 17-year-old girl named Molly Young. They were instructed to treat the children kindly and told that beatings were not condoned. Books were not used, but the children were educated through familiar conversation about common things. Flute music and marching were favorite activities, and the children heard stories and rhymes (Stewart, 1967).

Owen and his friend William Maclure were enthusiastic about the results of their enterprise. They studied the practices of Pestalozzi, who was then at the height of his popularity in his school at Yverdun, in Switzerland. Pestalozzi's sincere love of children and methods of teaching through perception were compatible with the ideas of these rich reformers. They began a second school in London, transferring Buchanan there as director. In 1826, they introduced their ideas to the United States by starting a third school in New Harmony, Indiana. Their aim was to provide children from two years of age through early childhood with lessons in the practical trades, in a kind of education distinguished by music and a spirit of joyfulness.

However, Owen did become particularly discouraged when, upon his return from New Harmony, he visited the London school and found Mrs. Buchanan terrorizing the children *and* her husband with a whip.

Although these early schools survived for only a few years, they led to the establishment of others. Evelyn Lawrence (1969, p. 34) has pointed out that the later experimenters, such as Samuel Wilderspin and David Stow, "developed schools which became increasingly didactic in tone, where the children's memories were exploited to the utmost and moral teaching was inculcated by every possible device."

In some way, Wilderspin took over Owen's London school, and there are reports that he and his wife, unassisted, superintended as many as 200 young children at one time. Then Mrs. Wilderspin died, and he began writing and lecturing on the infant school idea. He advocated a schoolroom for 200 children that was at least 80 feet long by 60 wide, with a tiered gallery at one end on which they sat to receive instruction. Lesson posts holding boards for six children and a monitor were arranged around the room; each post held a board that followed the lesson plans. Wilderspin advocated a great deal of outdoor play, in which his young charges were to choose their own occupations and manifest their characters; and he opposed what he termed "psitticism," a word derived from the Greek for parrot, which meant the mechanical repetition of lessons. His success is measured by the fact that by 1835 20,000 pupils were enrolled in about 300 infant schools of the United Kingdom (Wightman, 1860).

As the century wore on, women began to agitate increasingly for employment opportunities outside the "needle trades" and menial labor, and job opportunities in England began to increase. Although the "lower classes" had always expected the wife to work, little provision was made for care of their children. The situation became more acute when compulsory school laws forced older children into schools. The older children had to take the young ones along. It is estimated that 19,000 babies under three years of age were in schools during the mid-1870's, and of those aged three to five the total number rose from 1,179,228 in 1870 to 1,428,597 in 1900. While the total school population tripled, the enrollment of children under five was doubled (Whitbread, 1972, pp. 42-44).

Disruptive young children were often penned or tied into their seats, but as school populations increased it was necessary to build new classrooms for them; classrooms which promptly became overcrowded. An example is the Leicester elementary school infant building of 1893. Planned for forty children, it held double that number in five years (Whitbread, 1972, p. 45). There was an attempt to include an educational component. The baby class learned to speak clearly, to understand pictures, to recite the alphabet and to march to music. The five- to seven-year-olds in the Infant Class began reading and manual tasks. Since fifty or sixty children were often left with a girl 13 or 14 years old, the individualized Froebelian curriculum requiring a trained teacher could not be used. Also, this was a period of "payment by results" and there was administrative pressure to teach the three R's.

One aspect of child care which cannot be ignored is the joint emergence of the Victorian Lady and the governess. It was argued that a mother should not have to devote all her time to her children; she became a mother at scheduled times. Like the horsehair sofa, the nanny and the governess were part of the scenery. The nanny was only a servant, but the governess was considered a teacher and a lady. By 1851, there were 25,000 governesses in England; it is argued that the advances in women's rights were made possible because the time of educated and frustrated middle class and aristocratic women was sufficiently freed for "good works." Their role is discussed at length in a book whose title reflects the attitudes of the period, *Suffer and Be Still* (Vicinus, 1972, pp. 3-19).

In America, of course, problems were different. In colonial days, homeless children were taken in by relatives or friends. Poor families might be paid a dole to remain in their homes. About 1820, however, there was a change in attitude. Rothman (1971) attributes this to the belief held by legislators, philanthropists and government officials that society faced unprecedented dangers unless certain segments of the population were isolated. He calls this "the discovery of the asylum," since homeless children, the insane, the elderly poor and other unfortunates began to be taken care of in specially built institutions separate from the rest of society.

Meanwhile, some children from intact families were starting school at an early age—either dame school or public school. Reports from Boston dated 1819 detailed the duties and responsibilities of the schoolmistress for children aged four to seven. It is of interest to note that there was a ratio of 40 children to one teacher—unless she had a daughter old enough to help out. In that case, the salary was increased slightly and 80 children were assigned.

A graphic description of discipline in these early schools is found in Alice Earle's (1899) *Child Life in Colonial Days*. Street peddlers sold birch switches for babies and heavy walnut paddles for older and toughened schoolboys. There were ingenious punishments such as having a culprit cut a stick split so as to hold his own nose. Mrs. Earle describes the enforced precocity of children in the early days of America; they were taught to read English, Greek and Latin, and to memorize long portions of the Bible. One of these children, Timothy Dwight, not only learned to read the Bible before he was four, but taught it to "younger" children. He grew up to become president of Yale, but many of these young children died at an early age. Ms. Earle contends that the rigors and pressures of this type of education contributed significantly to the high mortality rate among young children of that era.

By the middle of the nineteenth century, New England had become heavily industrial. Large areas were populated by recent immigrants from Europe, with a heavy concentration of Irish. Humanitarian agitators, according to historian Merle Curti (1935), came from families in the ministry and other middle class groups, not from the industrialists whose annual profits might be 100 percent on their investment. The average length of life for the Boston Irish was 14 years. With one or two families per room and six or ten people per bed, there was little concern for child care outside the home. In the depression of 1837, one third of the population was unemployed; in 1884, one of eight persons was listed as a public pauper. Children aged 6 to 17 worked 11 hours or more, and the younger children frequently spent these hours inside the mill with their mothers. The common feeling was that this kept them out of mischief.

As the nineteenth century drew to a close, several trends affected young children and their parents. The massive influx of cheap immigrant labor, and the advance of machine technology, began to displace young children from factory work and provide an abundance of cheap domestic help. The rise of the Child Study movement, led by G. Stanley Hall and others, made the public more aware of children's needs and peculiarities. The Froebelian kindergarten, although only a half-day program in most cases, popularized the philanthropic role of prosperous young women who came face-to-face with the problems of their more unfortunate sisters.

The first organized day nurseries were a byproduct of ✓ the Civil War. In the Civil War, as in World Wars I and II, men went off to war, and the women were urged or forced to take their place in the industries they had abandoned, or to find work in war-related industries. So, in 1863, a permanent center was established in Philadelphia to take care of children whose mothers cleaned in the hospitals and manufactured soldiers' clothing. The French crèche was taken as a model for the original programs; later the Froebel kindergarten materials were incorporated into some centers. The movement grew slowly until about 1880, with private philanthropy financing care for only a few of the children whose mothers were forced to support their families. One result was that children were abandoned or surrendered to asylums. In 1899, New York City cared for 15,000 children at an expense of over one and one-half million dollars (Whipple, 1928, p. 92).

Both private individuals and public relief agencies became increasingly alarmed over the financial and emotional costs of full-time institutional care, and over the diversity of standards displayed by existing programs. In 1892, 90 regularly organized day nurseries were known of; by 1897, this number had almost doubled. The following year, these nurseries united under the National Federation of Day Nurseries, with offices in New York City (Whipple, 1928, p. 92).

As America entered the twentieth century, the need for day nurseries became even more apparent, more urgent and more difficult. The waves of European immigration supplied industry with more than enough cheap labor; because men's wages were not adequate for survival, women went to work too—and they earned even less money. The neglect of young children, which appalled industrial concerns as well as public-spirited citizens, led to a rapid expansion of day nursery programs. In turn, this explosion of programs led to such a drastic lowering of standards, even by well-intentioned relief agencies, that physicians and relief agencies were critical. It became generally assumed that provision of child care encouraged women to enter industry, and other forms of financial relief were investigated. Establishment of mothers' pension funds was suggested, the precursor to Aid to Needy Children, but was considered appropriate only for widows or other worthy females who were the sole support of their families.

As the need for day care became more obvious, a parallel development shut out one of the few avenues available to the concerned mother who either needed to work or who needed a few hours away from her young children. The kindergarten movement, in which both elite tuition classes and philanthropic free schools had been involved, was being taken over by public schools. In the past, children as young as two (or siblings who were still literally babies) had been admitted by Froebelian teachers—whose role often coincided with the role now assumed by social workers. However, school laws then began to exclude children below the age of six for first grade or five for kindergarten, and at the same time schools began to enforce compulsory attendance of the older children—children who, in the past, had been child-tenders for the younger ones. This left a great many very young children at loose ends. In Los Angeles, the situation was so critical that in 1917, the Board of Education established day care in the public schools with a 10¢ per day fee that almost covered expenses. No other city seems to have adopted this means of caring for young children (Whipple, 1928, pp. 90-91).

The situation at the turn of the century was abominable. It has not changed considerably since then, despite the vastly expanded knowledge of child development and awareness of educational needs. Too often, children remain in the modern equivalent of the antique dame school, in which there is some chance of a warm and positive environment, but in which there is just as much possibility of an environment that is harsh and sterile.

References

Ariés, P. *Centuries of childhood.* N.Y.: Alfred A. Knopf, 1962.

Braun, S. J., & Edwards, E. P. *History and theory of early childhood education.* Worthington, Ohio: Charles A. Jones, 1972.

Cole, M. *Robert Owen of New Lanark.* N.Y.: Oxford University Press, 1953.

Curti, M. *The social ideas of American educators.* N.Y.: Charles Scribner's Sons, 1935.

Earle, A. M. *Child life in Colonial days.* N.Y.: Macmillan, 1899. (18th printing, 1962.)

Gosden, P.H.J.H. *How they were taught.* Oxford, England:, 1969.

Lawrence, E. *Froebel and English education.* N.Y.: Schocken, (Reprinted 1969).

Raymont, T. *A history of the education of young children.* N.Y.: Longmans, Green & Co., 1937.

Rothman, D. J. *The discovery of the asylum.* Toronto & Boston: Little, Brown & Co., 1971.

Salmon, D. J. *Infant schools, their history and theory.* London: Longmans, Green & Co., 1904.

Stewart, W. A. A. & McCann, W. P., *The educational innovators.* N.Y.: St. Martin's Press, 1967.

Trexler, R. C. Infanticide in Florence: new sources and first results. *History of Childhood Quarterly,* Summer 1973, I (1), 98-116.

Vicinus, M. *Suffer and be still.* Bloomington: Indiana University Press, 1972.

Whipple, G. N. M. (Ed.) *The twenty-eighth yearbook of the National Society for the Study of Education.* Bloomington, Ill.: Public School Publishing Co., 1928.

Whitbread, N. *The evolution of the nursery-infant school.* London & Boston: Routledge & Kegan Paul, 1972.

Wightman, J.M. (Compiler) *Annals of the Boston primary school committee (1818-1855).* Boston: Geo. C. Rand & Avery, 1860.

Chapter Four

A BRIEF HISTORY
OF CHILD DEVELOPMENT
IN CALIFORNIA

Jeanada Nolan

At no period has there been so much attention—on both a state and national level—focused on child care and preschool education (now embraced in the term Child Development). For many years, educators have stressed the importance of the formative years—ages two to five—as the foundation for the child's development and later learning patterns. However, research findings were long overlooked or criticized until, relatively recently, governmental attention began to focus in programs such as Head Start and Title I of the Elementary/Secondary Education Act. The sudden public recognition that these research findings fit into the missing part of a pattern that seeks to explain the "why" of underachievers, dropouts and the "disadvantaged syndrome," has led to increased efforts to impress state and federal legislators with the need for child care and preschool education.

California has pioneered in programs of child care and preschool education since the early 1900's, when the State Department of Social Welfare began licensing nursery school and child care facilites. In the early 1920's parent participation preschools were developed under adult education, along with the development of private parent cooperative preschools.

The first government support to the field of child care was provided in the 1930's under the Works Progress Administration (WPA). Nursery schools were established that gave jobs to unemployed teachers and fed hungry children. Then, in 1942, federal Lanham Act funds became available for day care for children of working mothers on limited income so that these women might be available for the defense effort. Government support again became available in 1965 with the "War on Poverty" through Head Start, and later with the 1967 amendments to the Federal Social Security Act. These amendments made funds available for certain children who were federally eligible for child care or preschool programs. The Social Security legislation defined these programs as a public social service. A compensatory preschool educational program met one criterion of public social service because of its potential for strengthening family life.

CHILDREN'S CENTERS

During World War II, in the effort to meet manpower needs and to entice mothers into defense occupations, child care programs were established in the summer of 1942 with the federal Lanham Act funds. In California, these programs were initially under the auspices of the State Department of Social Welfare. However, in January 1943, the California Legislature, recognizing the educational importance of any program providing care for children, enacted a bill authorizing the establishment of a statewide child care center program, under the administration of the State Department of Education, operable through local school districts. The State Department of Social Welfare continued to provide consultant services as related to standards.

Three years later, when federal funding ceased, the

California Legislature adopted the principle of partial financial responsibility, with the parents of the children served paying fees based on a means test and a sliding scale. Until 1956, the Department of Education had to return to each legislative session to request continued funding for the next two years. In 1956 the program was adopted as a part of the state budget and it survived. In more recent years, some school districts have made available additional support to children's centers through local tax levies.

Other legislative modifications were made from time to time. A most significant action was taken in the 1965 session of the legislature. At that time, sections of the Education Code were amended, changing the title of this day care program from "Child Care Centers" to "Children's Centers," and the legislative intent was changed by rewording the description of the program from one that provided for "care and supervision" to one that provided for "supervision and instruction." Again the legislative mandate recognized that child care should be seen as educational as well as custodial. California is the only state that continued its funds to Children's Center programs from World War II to date. Since 1968, California has also utilized federal funds for welfare-linked children in child care from the Social Security Act.

COMPENSATORY PRESCHOOL PROGRAMS

The California Legislature in 1963 passed the McAteer Act, which paved the way for one of the most vital educational and social advancements in the history of California education. Dealing with the need for what it appropriately called "compensatory education," the Act recognized a serious problem in the American educational system and the need for special emphasis on upgrading educational services for children from "economically and culturally disadvantaged backgrounds."

The McAteer Act not only stressed the need for remedial measures for the disadvantaged, but embraced
preschool programs as a preventive measure.

The Department of Education since 1965 has operated a compensatory preschool program under contract
with the State Department of Social Welfare, which utilizes
federal Social Security funds for children of eligible
families. This program was facilitated by the passage in
1965 of the Unruh Preschool Act (AB 1331/65) which
added enabling legislation to both the Education Code and
the Welfare and Institutions Code that stated:

> The Legislature finds and declares that preschool
> programs with a strong educational component are of
> great value to all children in preparing them for success
> in school, and constitute an essential component of
> public social services. . . . The legislature further finds
> that such programs are often not available to many
> children who, because of the low income of their
> families, are deprived of this valuable experience.
> Therefore it is the intention of the legislature in enact-
> ing this chapter to provide equal educational opportun-
> ity to children of low income or disadvantaged families
> through appropriate arrangements for preschool of an
> educational value to be developed in accordance with a
> contractual agreement between the State Department
> of Social Welfare and the State Department of Educa-
> tion. The legislature believes that the introduction of
> young children to an atmosphere of learning will im-
> prove their performance and increase their motivation
> and productivity when they enter school. In order to
> achieve this end, all programs established under this
> chapter shall be centered upon a defined preschool
> educational program developed, conducted and ad-
> ministered with the maximum feasible participation of
> the families served by the program

In 1966 the Bureau of Preschool Education Programs, in the Office of Compensatory Education, State

Department of Education, was established to administer these programs. The Lewis Bill (AB 750), which was passed in 1970, made California the first state to provide for a statewide comprehensive and coordinated preschool and day care program modeled somewhat after the four C's concept (Community Coordinated Child Care). The Governor's Advisory Committee on Preschool Programs, established in the 1965 legislation, was expanded to provide for broader representation, including parents. This committee is known as the Governor's Advisory Committee on Child Development Programs. Although from the beginning public and private nonprofit agencies could be funded to operate the State Preschool Program, AB 750 made it possible to fund the private sector for preschool and child care. The passage of AB 734 (Braithwaite) approved conducting children's centers on college campuses. Subsequent passage of AB 99/72 (the Moretti-Brown-Lewis-Rodda Act) gave California a comprehensive child development program including family day care to be administered by the Department of Education. As a result of this, the Bureau of Preschool Education Programs was expanded to become a larger and separate Child Development Support Unit, which is now responsible for the State Preschool Program, children's centers, Title I (Elementary and Secondary Education Act, or ESEA) Preschool Component, Migrant Day Care/Preschool, the Migrant GROUP Infant Program and Campus Children's Centers. It has also been responsible for demonstration projects in child care emphasizing cost effectiveness and assuming responsibility for family day care formerly administered by the Department of Social Welfare through local County Welfare Departments.

Estimates indicate that as many as 500,000 disadvantaged preschool children in the state who could benefit from part-time or full-time preschool or child care programs if funding and facilities were available are not now serviced. With all of these programs, only about 67,000 children are currently being served. In spite of widespread interest, funds are being reduced and the need for programs is being questioned. The value of programs is being questioned, and the issue of cost effectiveness is being raised, mainly by the decision makers.

It has long been recognized that no matter what the preschool or child care program, no matter what the funding source, in order to be effective, and truly cost effective, the program must be educational in nature and soundly planned. It must contain the necessary components of health, nutrition, social services, educational planning, parent involvement, parent education, inservice education and evaluation. But what of evaluation?

Since 1965 both the Department of Education and the Governor's Advisory Committee on Child Development Programs have been making annual evaluation reports to the Legislature. Studies have quoted parents and program administrators as identifying preschool as one of the most desirable programs for building better home, school and community relations—and with reason. A recent evaluation of the State Preschool Program showed that within a seven month period between pre- and post-testing there was a mean mental age growth of 14 months and a mean growth in I.Q. equivalents of 17 points. Spin-off effects include positive changes in behavior of children and parents; changes in attitudes of parents; and parents returning to school to complete their own education.

The benefits of the state's Preschool Program have extended to entire families. As parents become involved, confidence and self-esteem are developed to the extent that many become employed or return to school and acquire the necessary skills to become economically independent. These are practical and realistic methods for upward mobility, for assisting the poor to break out of the poverty trap.

The use of aides from neighborhoods around the schools, in classrooms and in work with the children's parents, have opened up new career opportunities for young college students and graduates, as well as welfare parents. The programs have helped to "educate the educators" to the needs of children in welfare families. The program has brought the education and welfare systems more closely together in understanding the needs of deprived children and in focusing on the best ways to meet those needs.

Since 1970 the same emphasis on working with families and making all child care programs educationally sound has been taking place with similar findings. And now California has embarked on an Early Education Program which calls for restructuring or revitalizing the grades K through 3 while developing meaningful articulation with all of the existing preschool and child care programs in any given local school district embarking on the program. This includes joint planning and cooperation with nursery schools and day care, parent participation nursery schools, private parent cooperatives, institutional day care, etc. Many of the special features which have made the child development program successful are being incorporated into the kindergarten primary grades. The long-range goal is for the public schools in California to be able to offer an optional educational program for all four-year-olds, so that all children may benefit from an early developmental program.

REFERENCES

Bloom, B. S. *Stability and change in human characteristics.* N.Y.; John Wiley and Sons, Inc., 1964.

Early childhood development: alternatives for program implementation in the states. Denver: Education Commission of the States, 1971.

The early childhood education proposal: a master plan to redesign primary education in California. Sacramento: California State Department of Education, 1972.

Policies for early childhood education. Sacramento: California State Department of Education, 1973.

Report of the task force on early childhood education. Sacramento: California State Department of Education, 1972.

Chapter Five

THE DAY CARE
WORLD OF CHILDREN

Gertrude L. Hoffman

The intent of this paper is to present a warm, human, simple approach to one of the most profound problems of our times—that of the adequate care and supervision of children whose families need part-time supplementary help in carrying their responsibility for rearing children in a very complex world.

I venture to guess that many families are using maids, baby sitters, relatives, nursery schools or even a tightly programmed week of ballet lessons, music lessons, swimming, scouting and other structured programs to allow for time in which to pursue a profession, while, at the same time, maintaining a home in which children can flourish. I also venture that plans break down; maids don't come, relatives get sick, children become ill or school closes—and there is a scramble to find a substitute plan. These interruptions can reduce the security and stability of children's lives. Too many such episodes cause stress and tension, and the younger the children, the greater the risk.

I chose "The Day Care World of Children" as the title

Presented at the Annual Meeting of the American Medical Women's Association—November 9, 1970, San Juan, Puerto Rico.

for this paper because, for millions of children, some form and continuum of daily care by people other than their mothers is a way of life from birth through teens—in other words, their entire childhood. This constitutes the greater part of their world, and the quality of this day care world has a great influence, not only on each child but on the nation we are to become. Day care is of great importance for parents and children, but the impact on society is perhaps more significant. All of us, therefore, have a stake in this program.

So that we can function within the same framework, I am defining day care in my terms. Child care is technically an umbrella term which includes day care and covers all kinds of care and supervision of children. Day care usually means only care outside a child's own home in a day care center, a family day care home or in a small group home. Child care is not only these three but can be care in the child's own home, too. I am using child care and day care interchangeably because I want to present all forms of part-time care used by parents to supplement them in their child rearing responsibilities.

Day care is a very special service for children who must have supplementary care during part of the 24-hour day. They need this care because, for some reason, their parents are unable to provide care and supervision on a full-time basis. These parents do retain responsibility for their families, but need to delegate a part of this responsibility to others.

Since day care is a part-time substitute for parents in the totality of their child rearing, the distinguishing feature must be a degree of excellence surpassing all other daytime programs for children. In whatever setting the care is provided—a center, the home of a neighbor, in the child's own home or in a family day care home—the measure of excellence will be revealed in the degree to which the child is treated as an individual and the extent to which the care he receives meets his particular needs.

For some children, "nourishment" for meeting their

intellectual, physical, social and emotional growth and development needs can be provided in a day care center; for others, care in their own homes will provide greater stability and protection; for some, a family day care home where there are not more than one or two other children of the same age may be best; and for some, particularly from the same family or those of school age, the small group home may offer the most.

The essential purpose of child care is to provide a home base within which the child functions and from which he fans out into the larger society. It is the place where he can be himself, where he is accepted no matter what he does, where he can pursue his own interests and make his own friendships, the same as a child who operates from his own home with his mother providing the supervision. The providers of the direct care to the child must be equipped to offer him the same kind of opportunities as the best father and mother offer their children in the best possible home. This takes special insight and knowledge of child growth and development; it takes special interest in and a concern for and liking of children.

NEEDS OF CHILDREN

In order to draft a comprehensive community day care system to meet the needs of children and their families, we need, first, to review briefly what children are like in general at different ages and stages of their development. Then, we need to contemplate some of the individual circumstances that should be considered when deciding on the type of day care best suited to a particular child and his family.

When the 1967 amendments to the Social Security Act were passed and child care was required for public assistance recipients who registered for job training and subsequent employment, few new facilities opened. Children were often placed in whatever facility had an opening, usually with minimal intake requirements; or the nearest neighbor who would "mind the child" was pressed into service in order to expedite the parent's entrance into the labor market. Often these arrangements lasted only a short time. Either the parents gave up their training, or the child began the sorry treadmill of finding himself in a different place and with different faces every few days. We know of one child who came into a day care center at two years of age after a history of being in 22 different family day care homes.

While low-income families are more likely to suffer this kind of instability, not only in child care arrangements but in every facet of their existence, middle- and upper-income families also face many of the same problems. In an affluent society, it is especially hard to find people who can provide good quality child care. They are working at better paying jobs with more fringe benefits.

INFANTS AND TODDLERS

What is the most important thing infants need, want, and seek? The answer is a sense of security—of knowing that their world is O.K., that they can trust it. No one ever loses the need for this. All through life, we keep going back intermittently to reassure ourselves that the world is trustworthy. For infants and small children, the need is constant because the whole world is new.

It is at this very early stage of life that the child develops the capacity to form lasting interpersonal relationships. If there is no opportunity during the first 18 months of life to experience strong emotional ties with special adults who care for you, love you, play with you and encourage you, it is likely that relationships with others in the future will be impaired. This says a great deal to us who are planning and developing day care services for very young children.

The controversy has been raging for a long time about the appropriate setting in which good day care can be provided the infant and toddler. Many professionals—pediatricians, psychiatrists, social workers—and informed parents have steadfastly held that to care for infants in group care inherently denies the child the kind of individualized and continual attention that one person (his mother) or that one mother-substitute on a part-time basis could provide. This stems in part from research on the growth and development of infants reared in institutions, or the evaluation of children living in sterile surroundings with no toys, an impersonal staff which constantly changes or adults limited in their ability to talk and play with a child. Bowlby, Piaget, Skinner and others have varied in their assessment of types of facilities that care for children, but there is no basic difference in their assessment of the common human needs of infants.

Adults rightfully need to be on guard and concerned about the individualized care children need, but new research and investigation begin to tell us that it may be possible to build safeguards into different types of settings so that the dangers formerly attributed to the physical facility and its make-up need not exist.

If the essentials of good care are present, there is increasing evidence, although no proof, that the child can flourish in group care, or family care, or in his own home. The choice may need to be made on other measurements.

I am biased and feel that no day care center can be as home-like as a home. I feel children have a right to have the "run of the house," to learn not to touch a hot stove; to learn not to play with the dirty ash tray on the coffee table; to know the joy of older youngsters and their friends coming in after school with all the good-natured banter and horseplay.

Day care centers can offer children of all ages many things. But, I shudder at the thought of children spending all of their childhood in an institution. Therefore, I tend to lean toward the development of good family day care or the provision of adequate, trained caretakers in their own homes. I think combinations of types of care may be better for some children. For example, for many three-year-olds to have an adult in their own homes but go to Head Start or nursery school is far better than to share teachers, toys, and space with other three-year-olds for 10 or 12 hours a day.

Any institution moves on a schedule of some sort. For example, in a day care center, it would be difficult for a child who did not wish to go to the outdoor playground to stay in a day care center room by himself. He would have to conform to the schedule. In a family day care home with only three or four children and a backyard, the children can go in and out as they would in their own homes. An occasional check through the kitchen window assures they are all right, yet the children are not under the tension of constant adult surveillance. There may be more accidents and certainly more "getting into mischief," but there will be more learning, exploring and the satisfying of curiosity.

Several research projects indicate there are advantages and disadvantages in each kind of day care setting. For example, children may not learn language as well in a group setting where they must share the opportunity to talk and be talked to with others; in a home, the mother talks with the child, answers questions, and is available for conversation "on call." Centers, on the other hand, can provide far more social interchange, more varied experiences. They are also easier to monitor in terms of the controls over quality of staff and program content. Perhaps the best recent discussion of what a center can and cannot offer a young child has been written by Elizabeth Prescott (Pacific Oaks College, Pasadena, Calif.) as a result of her research in day care.

I suggest only that whatever the form of care, it be chosen because it fits the particular child and family situation, and offers the optimum potential for going simultaneously up the intellectual, emotional, physical and social growth path.

PRESCHOOL CHILDREN

Much less needs to be said about the care of preschool children—the three- through five-year-olds. Nursery school has become an acceptable and even an important social and learning experience for these children. Because of the child development and early childhood education disciplines, we know a great deal about the programming of a day in the day care center. Emphasis on the whole child has made it possible to offer a well-rounded daily program which is timed and tuned to the needs of the children. Most centers and nursery schools are full of educational, creative and stimulating playthings and equipment that entice not only the children but also their parents.

Parents tend to express a preference for nursery school or a day care center for their children because, in our society, learning is the single most important thing for children to engage in. I believe thoroughly, and desperately, that nursery school is a right—and not a privilege—for all children who can benefit from it. But, as I indicated in the beginning, day care is more than these programs.

Here I would like to examine for a few seconds the use of the 10- or 12-hour day in a nursery school setting as a day care plan for a three- or four-year-old child. At this age, the child is beginning to be a social creature. The interaction with others of his age is not only fun but also sets the stage for building good relationships with his peers throughout life. It exposes the child to all kinds of experiences. However, in evaluating day care plans for a child, there may be alternatives which do better for a particular child, or in a particular locale.

Ten or twelve hours a day is a long time to be in competition with your peers. It is a long time to share a teacher with three, four or five other youngsters your own age. It is a long day to have 15 or 20 people in the same room with you. Just the pressure of people and noise, even happy noise, can be wearing. If the child comes from a home where he must share his parents with too many siblings, perhaps another kind of day care plan would be better—maybe a good caretaker in the child's own home to care for all the children, but with whom the child spends several hours alone while the others are in school. Or perhaps he can use nursery school or Head Start for three hours, but not for ten; maybe a combination of in-home care or family day care and a short-time nursery school might be better.

With all the generalities that can be made about children—generalities upon which a program can validly be based—it is important to remember always that while much is the same in every child, there is also a unique, different and special part of each child that is unlike anyone else. Some learn quickly; others, slowly. Some display great sensitivity; others appear insensitive. Whatever the uniqueness, it should be preserved. The choice of day care, the planning on an individual basis for the right kind of care and combinations of care for each child will take extra work and insight on the part of parents, teachers, counselors and community. Certainly, all of us in the human professions have an obligation in whatever role we play to help assure that the child has his best chance in life.

Whatever the facility or in-home situation, knowledge of the needs and growth patterns of this age will help build into the setting the kind of programs that will protect against stress, yet will offer the opportunity to be fully "I." Day care, as a substitute for the child's home, is the key to the next step when the world truly opens up and the child goes forth.

SCHOOLAGE CHILDREN

Entry into kindergarten or first grade does not make a child suddenly into a new creature, without fear of new experiences, without need for adult support and, most especially, without the need for someone to be concerned about his well-being and to love him no matter what he does. The schoolage child has just as much need for the home base and substitute parent as does the preschooler or infant. He needs different degrees of attention, but to relegate this child to a group of 20 or 25 peer competitors after he has spent five or six hours in school with the same age group may be intolerable.

One of the grossest areas of neglect today is in the lack of care and supervision of schoolage children whose mothers are working or, for some other reason, are unavailable before and after school and on holidays and vacations. Too often, school becomes the day care plan. Even though the child may be on his own only an hour or so in the morning and two or three in the afternoon, the emotional impact of feeling that no one really cares where he is or what he does can be devastating. It is not possible to prove but it stands to reason that neglect and loneliness at this stage will take its toll sooner or later—in mental illness, in crime and delinquency, or in inadequate parenthood and an inability to love and be loved.

The schoolage child has many needs. Some can be met by community programs, some by individual planning for music or dance lessons and some through participation in organizations such as the YMCA, Boys Clubs, Scouts and Camp Fire Girls. None of these, however, takes the place of the special and constant adult to whom the child comes before and after school. Whether the child is in a day care center, a family home or in his own home, he needs to have freedom to be himself, he should not always have to be a part of a group. For most youngsters this age, the home-like base on his own street or at least in his own neighborhood is likely to be best. He can attend the same school his friends attend. He joins the kids in the street for marbles and has good relationships in the neighborhood.

Most day care programs that do exist for school children are day care centers. For the most part, they tend to overprotect and overschedule. The child is smothered by adults who direct and control his every movement. This not only insults the child, but does not provide the building blocks to maturity. New ideas for day care services are badly needed; new demonstrations are dreadfully lacking.

PRETEENS AND YOUNG ADOLESCENTS

Preteens are emancipated. At least they think so. And in many ways they are, but the sense of loneliness they feel when on their own is perhaps more devastating than for the younger child.

Preadolescence is the last stage of childhood and its importance for the future of the child is immense. A good day care program will afford the maximum opportunity for meeting the preadolescent's normal growth needs: freedom of choice, choice of friends, choice of activities, opportunities to explore the city and take trips and maybe even freedom to get a small job in which to earn money and esteem.

To plan day care services for the schoolage child or the preteen and early adolescent is a most difficult task. They rebel at authority and direction; take great delight in being rude, defiant, dirty and irresponsible. They may even seem devious. Conversely, they are exciting and venturesome, creative, expansive, friendly and pliable. During these years, individual talents assert themselves, special interests and skills come to the fore. Overprotection, too much adult planning and scheduling, too many prescribed programs deny the child a chance to create his own entertainment and fun, deny him the joy of seeking knowledge without pressure and make him too dependent on others in designing his own style of life. A good day care program will create the safeguards appropriate to the degree of maturity of each child and will encourage and assist him to take the next giant step on his own, falling back on adult support, concern and interest when he needs it.

Types of Facilities

Generally, a community needs four types of care, or facilities. One or more of these may be used at a given time, and the same child, over a period of 12 or 15 years, may use each kind of facility.

A *day care center* is the type of facility best understood by the general public, although its purpose and function are often misunderstood. A center usually cares for children in groups of peers and sorts them according to age and special need. However, a good center provides opportunity for the experience and learning that accompany a mixing of ages, at least for part of the day. Centers are especially suitable for the preschool child three through five years of age. They may also meet the needs of many schoolage children.

The *family day care home* usually serves a few children (five or six). The home actually is that of a family other than the child's own, but the person caring for the children carries on much as a mother would in her own home.

Good family day care should come under the supervision and aegis of some agency or organization with experience in this field. At the present time, however, most family day care homes are informally established. A mother finds a neighbor who will care for her children. The neighbor may or may not care for other children. Many of these homes are licensed or approved by a State agency. This assures that the home meets certain physical requirements such as square footage per child, adequate plumbing and outdoor space. A few licensing requirements attempt to set standards for personnel, usually in terms of minimum and maximum age, "good physical and mental health," and perhaps a minimum of schooling.

Few such homes have caretakers who have had any training or ongoing supervision. Although very good care is being offered many children through this system, it is one which easily breaks down, and the mother finds herself in the position of having to find anybody who can fill in so she can keep her job.

I believe good family day care is an excellent and preferred method of care for many children. The caretaker
should receive adequate compensation, and be required to
take training so she knows something about good child
growth and development, as well as about kinds of toys and
play equipment. She must understand the importance of
language and her role in fostering its development. She
should have sick leave, vacations and substitutes on call so
that care is uninterrupted for the child and his mother, and
so that she can have some ongoing training. There should
be a separate fund for food and creative toys.

This kind of care will probably not be cheaper than
group care. It will just be more suitable for some families
and for some neighborhoods, and it can offer the child a
relaxed, homelike setting in which to develop at his own
pace.

A *small group home* is one in which 12 or 15 children can
be cared for and in which they can operate much as they
would in and from their own homes. It seems to me this is
particularly good for schoolage children or young teenagers. The small group home should have at its helm a staff,
preferably a couple, who act in lieu of parents for part of
the day. They are there each day, offering stability, guidance, concern and interest, but they do not smother the
child with routine prescribed activities. In this kind of setting, each child can have his own friends, visit their homes,
bring a friend home with him, spontaneously decide he will
go swimming or shoot marbles with the gang in his street.
He can choose to play with the others in the facility, get help
with his homework, look at a special television show. Boys
and girls get individual attention and guidance but are not
forced to function en masse. People directing these homes
should have special training and understanding of school
age children. The homes should be under the administration and supervision of community agencies or organizations so that the staff may have the benefit of support and
consultation by professional personnel. Deep involvement

of parents and children in the operation and administration is extremely important.

The small group home is excellent for families with several siblings. It keeps the children together, yet places no undue responsibility on older children to care for younger ones. In this kind of home, preteens could be paid to help with the younger children. During the long summer days, youngsters could participate in a number of activities in the community.

The small group home is a new concept. Baltimore, Maryland is about to establish some of these homes in its Model Cities neighborhoods.

The day care center, the family day care home and the small group home are the traditional kinds of group day care. The fourth kind of care is in the child's *own home* by someone other than his mother. It may be a relative, a maid, a baby sitter, an older sibling or anyone the mother can find who will look after the children and perhaps do some of the housework. Actually, this is the most common kind of care the working mother uses. More than 50 percent of the children in care are in their own homes.

I believe this form of child care to be most appropriate for many children, and that, as a society, we should assure training and supervision for people who come into the home to care for children. Parents should be able to have competent people who choose to care for children because they love them and who have the necessary training and experience.

STATUS OF CHILD CARE

It is essential that there be a change in the status of child care in this country. We are far behind Western Europe in our national commitment to children. In other countries, there is status in becoming a caretaker of children. In the Scandinavian countries, and also in Russia, great importance is placed on the quality of day care; every person providing such must have training.

Until this nation is willing to pay adequately for caretakers and truly faces the reality that its future depends wholly on the quality of the life of its children, we will continue to shortchange our youngest citizens and create insurmountable problems for the future.

THE SIZE OF THE PROBLEM

There are about 20 million children whose mothers are already in the labor market. For the most part, these children are *not* from the lowest economic level where parents may need job training and subsequent employment, or who may be required to enter training and the labor market because they are currently receiving public assistance. At present there are about 639,000 places for children in licensed day care facilities in this country. Approximately 518,000 children are in day care centers and 120,000 in family day care homes. Thus, regardless of the numbers of children cared for in their own homes or by relatives, the gap between need and available facilities is shocking.

Statistics such as these do not tell the story of quality. They do not tell of nonlicensed facilities which may be doing a very good job but just do not fall under the legal mandate for regulation. But even if we could count all of these, the obvious dearth of care for children leads me to say that I believe we must utilize every avenue for the development of new facilities, launch extensive training programs for all kinds of personnel and entertain involvement of small commercial enterprises, big business, voluntary agencies and organizations, as well as public agencies in creating good, new, day care programs for children. These should be of many kinds and varieties to meet individual needs, but all must assure adequate health, education and social services according to the need of each family so that no child is cheated of his opportunity to grow in the best way possible. Currently, there is no way to finance such services from one source. Public money, private philanthropy, parents' fees, business involvement and combinations of all these will be needed to grapple effectively with such a mass problem.

FUNDING SCOURCES

Under current [as of November 1970] federal statutes, money is available from several sources for day care of children. The technicalities involved in utilizing these funds are many and cannot be discussed at this time. I shall list only major sources of funds and briefly say how they can be used. The largest appropriation is through Title IV-A of the Social Security Act, which provides 75 percent reimbursement to state public welfare agencies for expenditures for child care for children whose families receive assistance under the Aid to Families with Dependent Children program, or who formerly received such aid or who might for some reason need AFDC within the next five years. Many of these children have parents enrolled in the Work Incentive (WIN) program, although large groups are in day care because their parents were already employed, or because their families are extremely disadvantaged and the children need early intervention to enable them to function in the larger society.

Head Start provides day care centers on a full-time basis in many communities. This is limited to children whose families are at or below the poverty level, except for 10 percent whose incomes may be higher. Currently, this program serves about 78,000 children. These two programs are administered by the Department of Health, Education and Welfare. The Special Food Service for Children program, administered by the Department of Agriculture, can provide food for low-income children in day care centers.

A program of research and demonstration in the day

care field with an allocation of several million dollars was operated by the Office of Economic Opportunity during 1970-72. The Department of Labor supports some day care services as a backup for various manpower programs.

The Department of Housing and Urban Development offers help in the construction of facilities through its Neighborhood Service program, through provision of facilities in public housing projects and through use of Model Cities supplemental funds in those communities designated as Model Cities neighborhoods.

Legislation has been pending in the Congress for some time and would change the child care picture considerably. One major piece was former President Nixon's Family Assistance Plan (FAP) or the Welfare Reform Act. Without giving the details of the bill, I would like to point out that it carried a large child care program for children of those eligible for FAP and for some who had been receiving child care under the Work Incentive program. It has been estimated that about 348,666 schoolage children and 174,333 preschool children would receive child care under the FAP program. An amendment proposed by Senator Long was to establish a national agency to build centers, and set standards and administer child care of all kinds.

In addition, Title IV of the Social Security Act will continue to provide child care for many low-income children not eligible for care under FAP.

There are several other major bills (Brademas, Abzug, Dellenbach, Mondale and others) which have been introduced and have had hearings but have not progressed beyond that stage. All of them are considered comprehensive child development bills and provide, in addition to day care, for services to all preschool children regardless of income. They also carry provision for construction of facilities.

Enactment of any legislation still will not solve all the problems, nor deliver child care services to all the children and families that need them. We do need public commitment and federal, state and local funds. But we also need commitment from business and industry, from concerned citizens, from the currently operating groups, commercial and voluntary, from labor groups and particularly and especially from parents of children in need of good care, in order to help put together a unique, workable delivery system that will provide a network of child care services in every county in the country. By no means can one organization mount such a system on its own, but it seems imperative that one of the institutional programs take leadership and major responsibility for consolidation of effort because only such an institution has access to the already existing agencies that cover the entire country. I happen to believe the public welfare department is the logical agency to provide this leadership. It is the agency charged with assuring the availability of child welfare services to all children who need them wherever they live. Child care is a child welfare service primarily because it is a supplement to families in providing care, supervision and guidance of children. It is not primarily an education or health service, although both these components must be included in a good child care program. However, if some other institution can do the job better, I would support that institution.

Whatever the aegis, whatever the administration and regardless of the source of funds, communities must be involved in establishing the quality of service that children need, in monitoring the delivery system and in helping parents and guardians to avail themselves of the best possible care for their children.

THE ROLE OF THE PHYSICIAN

It seems to me that physicians have several special roles to play in the delivery of day care services. Of course, the general standards-setting of health services and health programs for child care facilities should stem from the medical knowledge and skill of the bonafide physician.

Administering agencies must have access to consultation from at least one physician, although it is preferable to be able to ask the medical society to set reasonable and effective health requirements for all programs. In addition, individual health screening, follow-up medical and dental treatment and preventive health care are essential for many children.

The individual physician needs to know what the different types and styles of day care facilities can offer children so that he is able to help a family make a good plan of care when his advice is needed. Specialists from the medical field will be needed as consultants to programs such as those for retarded children and the physically handicapped. All programs need consultation from psychiatrists, on occasion. The general practitioner and the pediatrician are essential partners with social workers and educators in assuring that health, education and social service components are meeting the needs of the children.

My final plea is that you become acquainted with the child care in your community and join forces with others to create more opportunities for children to have good day care. Make it possible for parents to have a real choice about their own employment and satisfactions, both as parents and as working members of society. It is equally important to make it possible for the mother who wants to stay at home with her children to do so, because she chooses this as her vocation.

REFERENCES

Bowlby, J. *Maternal care and mental health*. Geneva: World Health Organization, 1952.

Yarrow, L. Separation from parents in early childhood. In M. L. Hoffman & L. W. Hoffman (Eds.), *Review of child development research*. Vol. I. N. Y.: Russel Sage Foundation, 1965, pp. 89-136.

Provence, S. *Guide to the care of infants in groups.* N. Y.: Child Welfare League of America, Inc., 1967.

Piaget, J. *The origins of intelligence in children.* N. Y.: International Universities Press, 1952.

Piaget, J. *The construction of reality in the child.* N.Y.: Basic Books, 1954.

Prescott, E. *Children in group day care: the effect of a dual child rearing environment.* Los Angeles: Welfare Planning Council.

A pilot study of day care centers and their clientele. Washington, D.C.: Department of Health, Education, and Welfare, Children's Bureau, 1965.

Chapter Six

GETTING ORGANIZED FOR CHILD DEVELOPMENT SERVICES

Jule M. Sugarman

THREE STAGES OF ORGANIZING

Creating a comprehensive child development program involves three separate stages. These are:

I. Establishing a legal framework including establishing service areas; creating a policy body; enacting legislation or issuing regulations; and, selection an administering agency.
II. Preparing a comprehensive child development plan.
III. Developing, approving and supervising projects.

While the three stages may overlap to some degree, they are for the most part sequential. That is, one stage must be completed before going on to the next.

SERVICE AREAS

One of the first decisions the organizers of a comprehensive program must make is how to define service areas. The first major question involves achieving geographic compatibility between the state-oriented Title IV programs and the locally oriented Head Start and Elementary and Secondary Education Act programs. In the proposed federal child development act the device of a prime sponsor accomplished this. Local governments were given the prime responsibility in certain areas and the state government in the remaining areas. Determining the minimum population a local government had to have in order to qualify as a prime sponsor generated considerable controversy. The 1971 version of the act set the minimum at 5,000; the 1972 version at 25,000. Various critics argued for 100,000, 250,000 or 500,000.

Most commentators did agree, however, that the eligible types of local governments should include cities, counties or other units of general local government. Boards of education or other organizations that do not have general governmental powers were not eligible. On Federal Indian reservations, tribal councils could serve as prime sponsors. (The state government was to be the prime sponsor of child development programs in those areas where neither a local government nor a tribal council had been approved, or where HEW had not approved an application by the local government.) If two local governments, e.g., a city and a county, applied to be prime sponsor for the same area, the Office of Child Development (OCD) would have had the authority to determine which local government could serve the area more effectively. OCD would also have been required to encourage local governments to combine their applications if they could not be effective operating alone.

In the absence of federal legislation clearly the states must make the decisions as to the size and nature of administrative areas. These decisions should take into account the following factors:

1. The minimum size of area that may be necessary to

support a viable comprehensive program. This means that the program must be large enough to (a) justify a full central staff including necessary specialists, and (b) permit a variety of programs (e.g., part- and full-time programs, special services for handicapped children, etc.).

2. The feasibility of active parent participation.
3. The degree to which local support including financing may be available. The availability of local private or public funds for the nonfederal share may be a critical factor.
4. The relative potential bureaucratic competence of state and local units of government to carry out programs.
5. Considerations of cultural and ethnic differences.
6. Existence of other planning or administrative areas such as those required by the Federal Government.
7. Relationship to employment service and welfare department requirements and organization for day care under the work incentive (WIN) program.
8. Other regional cooperative arrangements.

It is my opinion that a program ought to anticipate serving at least 1,000 children in order to be established as a separate administrative service area.

It should be borne in mind that arrangements can be devised whereby local governments would have substantial input on policy even though the state government administered programs in their area. For example, the 1972 Act provided for local advisory councils for each local service area appointed by local officials and parents. These service areas generally were to include a maximum of 50,000 persons. The local advisory council had real power in developing the comprehensive plan and in approving project applications.

It should also be borne in mind that the general trend

of congressional action is to give greater authority and funding to large local governments rather than requiring all funds to flow through the states. Examples of this may be found in the Revenue Sharing Act, the comprehensive manpower leiglsation and the Allied Services Act (for social services).

Finally, it should be clear that no arrangement for child development will be fully compatible with other systems. They simply are not compatible with one another. Planning areas do not correspond with social service areas, nor do health and education service areas match. Whatever arrangement is chosen for child development will have to find ways to bridge to other geographic arrangements.

For example, if the child development service area is based on welfare department structure, it may be necessary to form a special advisory committee of local school districts in areas covered by the welfare department. Similarly,if the joint administrative unit used by the employment service and the welfare department covers different areas, a child development procedure will have to be created for interchange among them.

Local and state laws vary regarding the source of authority to determine whether a local government will operate as a local services area. In some jurisdictions, the chief executive officer—that is, the mayor, the chairman of the board of county commissioners, or the town supervisor—may act on his own authority. In other jurisdictions, the legislative body—that is, the city council, the full board of county commissioners or town supervisors, or the state legislature—may have to act. Some state laws do not permit local juridsictions to initiate new programs or organizations without authorization from the state legislature. Legal advice on these matters should be obtained from the local corporation counsel, town or county attorney, or the state attorney general. The legal counsel in the HEW regional office also may be helpful.

The Child Development Council and Agency: the First Steps in Creating a Comprehensive Plan

I believe that parents, experts and other knowledgeable individuals should participate actively in every stage of developing a comprehensive program. Specifically, such participation ought to take place before decisions are made about legislation, the size of administrative service areas and the agency to administer the program. This means that the governor, mayor or other local officials ought to appoint an advisory planning committee to assist in the initial planning of a comprehensive program. Such a committee ought to include substantial representation from parents with children in these programs. If at all possible parent organizations, rather than the governor or mayor, should select parent representatives. Representatives of institutions of higher education also should participate, since training is so critical..

The advisory group ought to be broadly representative of the general public and include government and private agencies in such fields as economic opportunity, health, education, welfare, employment and training, as well as business or financial organizations or institutions, labor unions and employers.

SETTING UP THE COUNCIL

Ordinarily the chief executive will take the initiative in creating an advisory planning committee. However, local groups may wish to make proposals designed to encourage him to act. Regardless of who takes the first initiative, it is important that the plan for an advisory planning committee be developed in a way that will permit full public discussion. The following steps are suggested:

1. A public meeting is convened to which are invited representatives of all existing child development

programs (parents and staff), employers or labor unions interested in day care, officials of minority organizations, church leaders and professional and academic persons who are experts in child development. Among those who should be invited are pediatricians, child psychologists, dentists, public health nurses, optometrists, early childhood educators, social workers and home economists, as well as public officials from education, health, mental health, welfare and other pertinent agencies.

In some states or local communities 4-C (Comprehensive Coordinated Child Care) groups already exist for the purpose of planning. HEW has encouraged the creation of these groups as a way of starting coordinated planning under legislation that previously had been passed. It would be logical to use such a coordinating group as the nucleus for planning. The regional OCD can advise as to whether there is a 4-C group in your community.

2. The governor or mayor's staff should prepare an outline describing the existing situation, and the problems, opportunities and proposed composition of the planning committee

3. At the first meeting this outline should be explained and questions and comments should be received. Before the meeting ends there should be agreement on the procedures by which the planning committee will be appointed.

4. The governor or mayor should arrange for paid or volunteer staff to work with the planning committee. Staff is essential in seeing that the job gets done. OCD or the state government may be able to provide technical assistance to such staff or to finance consultant staff to assist in drawing up the proposal. Check with the regional Office of Child Development in the Department of Health, Education, and Welfare.

5. The planning committee ought to make recommendations on these questions:

A. *What programs should be considered as a part of the comprehensive child development program (e.g., Head Start, Title IV, ESEA, etc.)?*
B. *What will be the number of parent members? Which public and private organizations will be represented on a permanent child development council? What will be the number of expert representatives?* The planning committee should not seek the names of specific individuals for the council unless the chief executive or legislative body so requests. Rather it should identify the kinds of organizations which ought to be represented. There may be more organizations interested than there are seats on the council. In that case, the planning committee may want to consider interest groupings—for example, all organizations interested in child health, all black minority groups or all early childhood educator groups. One of the issues that must be faced is whether the representatives of various interested groups are to be selected by those groups themselves or whether the chief executive will be free to select a person wholly of his choice. The governor or mayor really has the deciding voice on this question, since the laws give them power of appointment. A chief executive may, however, be willing to voluntarily restrict himself to persons nominated by the interest groups. Chief executives may also want to rotate membership among various organizations within an interest group. For example, if there is to be only one space for a religious representative it might be rotated among the faiths.
C. *What method will be used for initial selection of parent members?* The alternatives include:
   —Selection of delegates to a convention by each funded program; the convention will then in its turn select council members.

—A convention of all parents to select members directly.

—A convention of all parents to elect delegates who will then select council members.

Parent members should be appointed by the chief executive, although it would be desirable once the comprehensive program is fully organized to make parent appointments almost automatic when they have been elected by the parents.

D. *What organizations will be chosen to administer the program?* The fundamental question is whether there should be simply a coordinating organization as in the 4-C model, or whether a new or existing agency should be given responsibility for the program.

The planning committee makes it recommendations to the chief executive officer or legislative body. They of course are legally free to accept, modify or reject them.

ESTABLISHING THE LEGAL FRAMEWORK. EXECUTIVE ORDER OR LEGISLATION

Once the governor or mayor has received the recommendations of the advisory planning committee he must decide what legal steps he wishes to take to carry out the recommendations. If he opts for a coordinating committee approach he probably can accomplish this simply by issuing an executive order or similar regulation.

The executive ought at a minimum to specify:

—The functions of the coordinating organization;

—The composition of the policy advisory committee and the methods for appointing members.

—The source of funding for the staff and the method for appointing staff.

—Those organizations which are required to participate in or cooperate with the coordinating organization;

—In the case of a state organization, the relationship with local coordinating organizations.

—The reports required.

In addition, the governor or mayor may want to set specific work goals for the coordinating organization. For example, he may ask that it develop within one year a statewide training program or a coordinated system of licensing and inspection.

If the chief executive wishes to create or designate an agency for child development, he probably will need legislation. In some cases governors or mayors have the authority to do this as a reorganization plan, but the plan usually has to be approved by the legislature. Whether new legislation or an executive order is required, the same substantive points must be covered.

—The scope of programs to be included in comprehensive child development.

—The administrative organization or organizations and the authorities and responsibilities to be assigned them.

—The methods of financing, including any necessary authorities to transfer funds among organizations;

—The membership and authority of the child development council;

——The obligations imposed on other departments to cooperate with the child development agency;

—The process for establishing local service areas and advisory child development committees for them.

—The authority of local governments to establish comprehensive child development programs; the degree of state supervision; the nature of state financial support; and the nature of cooperation between state and local agencies.

A model child development law is being developed by

the Education Commission of the states. An alternative version has been prepared by the author of this chapter.

The development of local legislation would be similar to the process at the state level. It should be clearly understood however that local government

—may enact only such legislation as the state constitution and laws authorize them to enact;

—must enact legislation which is compatible with state arrangements for federal programs such as Title IV, Head Start and ESEA.

A critical factor in both state and local legislation is, of course, Title IV. Federal law requires that it be administered by a single state agency—the state welfare department. A governor may request the Secretary of HEW to approve use of a different agency (e.g., a child development agency). In the case of local agencies, states have the authority to (and many already do) delegate administration of child development programs to local governments.

States and local communities are advised to consult closely with regional HEW officials before acting on legislation, in order to assure that federal mandates are being met.

TYPICAL FUNCTIONS OF A CHILD DEVELOPMENT AGENCY

—Prepare the annual comprehensive child development plan;

—Plan, supervise, coordinate, monitor and evaluate child development programs in the prime sponsorship area;

—Contract with public or private non-profit and for-profit agencies or organizations to operate programs;

—Contract or otherwise arrange with state, local, or private non-profit organizations for: child-related family, social and rehabilitative services; coordination with educational agencies; health, mental

health, and family planning services; nutrition services; training or personnel;
—Conduct hearings on project applications.

OPERATION OF THE PERMANENT CHILD DEVELOPMENT COUNCIL

Once the chief executive or legislative body has appointed the members of the child development council, the
council must organize itself. The child development council
may elect its own chairman or the chairman can be named
by the chief executive. In order to function, the council
needs to establish a set of bylaws, a work plan and procedures for its operation. Before examining each of these
areas we should consider certain general matters.

The most difficult problem the council will face in the
early days will be to define a clear division of responsibility
between the council and the administering agency. This
may be either an existing agency or a newly created agency.
The council must understand that there are limitations on
the number of matters with which it can deal. Its members
often have full-time jobs and usually are not paid for council work. As a rule of thumb, the work of the council and its
committees ought not to require an average of more than
12 hours a month. The council often can save time by doing
much of its work through committees which are able to
speak on behalf of the council. Such committees should,
however, be representative of the composition of the council, including the appropriate proportion of parent membership.

The standing committees and their functions probably
will be more or less as follows:

Executive Committee—Empowered to act on behalf of
the entire council between meetings. The limitations
on the powers of the executive committee should be
spelled out. For example, it probably should *not* have
authority to approve the annual child development

plan, to change the bylaws or to approve fund allocations, since these are all decisions critical to the work of
the council.

Program and Facilities Standards—Studies and recommends supplements to federal program and facilities
standards. Would include staffing standards, hours of
service, types of health and social services, work and
play space, etc.

Personnel Policies and Career Development—Studies and
recommends personnel qualifications, methods for re-
cruiting and examining of staff, salary levels, promotion ladders, staff training, labor relations policies, uses
of volunteers, and all other matters related to employment.

Facilities Planning—Studies and recommends need for
new facilities. Explores alternative methods for obtaining space by lease, remodeling or construction. Makes
recommendations to council.

Appeals and Grievances—Recommends policies and
procedures on handling of grievances and appeals.
Conducts hearings on those matters that must be heard
by the council (e.g., decisions by the child development
agency to suspend a project or a serious complaint by a
parent).

Program Performance—Reviews monitoring reports,
makes independent visits to operating programs to
determine whether they are operating in accordance
with approved policies, makes recommendations to
councils.

Research and Planning—Studies and recommends
evaluation systems; approves outside requests for
permission to conduct research projects; considers
ideas for new types of programs to be developed in the
future. Plans annual seminar and program ideas.

Project Policy Committee Liaison—Meets regularly with project policy committees to explore their views and concerns.

Comprehensive Child Development Plan—Works with administering agency to develop and update annual child development plan.

Within available time limits the council must choose the most important matters for its consideration. Among these matters are:

—Consideration of candidates for director of the child development agency;
—Approval of the annual child development plan;
—Holding of hearings on project applications (although this may be done by a committee);
—Fund allocations among areas;
—Policies on types of programs to be financed;
—Program standards;
—General personnel policies;
—Hearing of grievances and complaints involving major issues of policy;
—Review of overall program performance;

Other types of matters that are probably more directly the responsibility of the director of the child development agency are:

—Appointment of all subordinate officials;
—Development of instructions for submission of project applications;
—Review and approval of project applications unless a hearing is requested;
—Preparation of recommendations on fund allocations, program standards, personnel policies;
—Internal administrative organization and policies for the child development agency;

—Handling of complaints and grievances which do not involve major issues of policy;

—Labor negotiations;

—Approval of qualifications for key appointees in funded projects;

—Routine monitoring of performance by project sponsor and initiation of corrective action;

The work of the council can also be greatly expedited if materials are prepared in writing and submitted well in advance for its consideration. These materials should provide the council with all relevant facts and should describe both the recommended decision and possible alternatives.

The council may wish to obtain advice on some matters from persons outside the child development agency. Funds should be reserved for the hiring of consultants by the council. In larger cities the volume of work may require that the council have a full-time staff of its own.

It is essential that the council have a set of bylaws governing its operation. The council should also ask the child development agency or its own staff to develop an annual work plan. Knowing what it has to do well in advance will greatly help a council to get its work done.

The handling of serious complaints and grievances is one of the council's most difficult duties. The public's perception of the way in which it does this job can vitally affect the degree of public support. The council must balance the need for sensitivity and compassion towards the rights of complainants with the need to assure orderly and proper operation of programs. Essential to the proper handling of complaints and grievances is a set of written policies which clearly define the right to appeal and the procedures under which appeals will be considered.

Chapter Seven

PROFITING FROM DAY CARE

William L. Pierce

The expansion of day care in the United States has been my specific study for more than two years. The most controversial and persistent issue that kept coming up was the question of the profit motive as it applies to human services and, more specifically, to that human service we call "day care." During this time, the related question has arisen as to whether day care could expand into a "big business," or whether it should be considered a "public service."

On examination, day care is no different from other human services. Profiting from day care is really no different from profiting from other human and welfare services for children such as adoption or foster care. Profiting from human services for children is the same as profiting from services to people of all ages.

During the last two years, the subject of profiting from human services has been discussed relatively little. One of the few recent books which focuses on the question, Richard Titmuss's (1970) *The Gift Relationship*, has not had the impact it should have had. The book deserves fuller consideration and appreciation. Titmuss discusses the relationship between human values and human services in the context of the provision of human blood. Perhaps the need for blood is far enough removed from most people's experience that Titmuss's argument seems academic, almost irrelevant. Only a tiny minority of the population is directly affected during any one year by decisions concerning the provision of blood.

There are other "human services" that directly and constantly affect almost the entire population. Perhaps it would have more impact to examine one of these more widespread services, in that the need to provide human services in this field is universally recognized.

One such area is in the field of health; sufficient attention has been focused on the failures of the present health system so that the debate is not about whether there shall be a "national health plan," but about what the "national health plan" will look like. Suggested plans ranged from the "catastrophic health plan" of Russell Long, Chairman of the Senate Finance Committee, through the more generous, even better plan proposed by Senator Edward Kennedy and Congresswoman Griffiths, to the National Health Plan that has been developed by the Medical Committee for Human Rights. The Medical Committee for Human Rights, whose plan has been endorsed by Congresswoman Shirley Chisholm (1972) among others, believes that "health care is a right not a privilege." Once that premise and all that it implies is accepted it is possible to see the MCHR's (undated) guidelines for a national health plan as the next logical step. The guidelines are:

1. Make health care a service, not a profit-making business;
2. Pay for all health care services with a progressive tax on total wealth—personal and corporate;
3. Administer medical centers locally through representatives of patients and health workers;
4. Provide complete and preventive health care with no charges for health services;

5. Create a federal nonprofit corporation to produce and distribute drugs and medical supplies.

"Education" is a human service that is even more universal. Nearly everyone in the country is either a student, the parent of a student or a taxpayer who supplies part of the money necessary to provide for teachers, classrooms and equipment.

Few people do not fit into one or more of these categories. "Education" is such a pervasive human service that even persons who have completed their education and who have decided to raise no children are still involved with education, through taxes. A large portion of property taxes, for instance, generally goes toward education. But even if a person owns no real property, he is still, as of 1972, involved in paying for education in a substantial way. Through the federal tax system (Conner & Ellena, undated; *Washington Star,* 1972), we are now providing eight percent of the funds for preschool education, seven percent of the funds for elementary and secondary education and thirteen percent of the funds for higher education. One member of Congress who is extremely influential in the area of education financing, has set as a goal that the government should finance 35 percent of all education costs from kindergarten through college *(Washington Star,* 1972).

The entire population will be similarly "involved" with education—by helping to pay for it—if any version is adopted of the Value Added Tax that had been discussed by the Nixon Administration and others as a potential financing mechanism for education. Such a "national sales tax" touches everyone.

Part of the reason that the impact of education is so widespread is that this country has already moved beyond the concept that "education is a right not a privilege." While it is true, as John Knowles (undated) says, that "medical care in this country is not a public responsibility," a certain amount of education is seen as a public responsibility. For a certain number of years in the life of every person education is not only a right, but also a duty —education is compulsory.

Given the fact that it is our national policy that education is a right and not a privilege, it should be no surprise to anyone that, at least in funding, our educational practice is beginning to shudder and shake its way into conformity with our educational posture.

It is interesting and informative at this point to take another look at the "medical" guidelines proposed in the five-point plan of the Medical Committee for Human Rights, but this time substitute the word "education" for the words "medical" and "health":

1. Make education a service, not a profit-making business;
2. Pay for all educational services with a progressive tax on total wealth—personal and corporate;
3. Administer educational centers locally through representatives of students, parents and educational workers;
4. Provide complete and preventive education with no charges for educational services;
5. Create a federal nonprofit corporation to produce and distribute books and educational supplies.

A position that seemed radical when applied to health, seems only reasonable when applied to education; however, once one accepts the premise that education is not only a right but a public responsibility, few alternatives seem logical. And we seem to be moving in that direction in regard to health care.

However, while education is accepted as a public responsibility and the country does seem to be tending toward treating health as a public responsibility, that variety of services we put under the catch-all term "welfare" is faring very differently. Under the slogan "welfare reform" a series of steps is being proposed that would undo much of what has been accomplished in the area of health and go a long way toward repudiating any practical possibility of carrying out the avowed national policy on education. These backward steps are being taken as a part of a general retreat from the idea that welfare is a public responsibility.

The attacks on the concept that welfare is a public responsibility are coming from all quarters. Democrats and Republicans of all shades of opinion have been joining in endorsing the "welfare reform" bill as part of what Vermont Royster (1972), in the *Wall Street Journal,* calls chronic "me-tooism." Even among the national voluntary organizations and the powerful lobby groups, "me-tooism" on welfare has been the rule.

There are voices of organizational dissent that can be heard in the midst of the chorus of "me-tooing." Most opposition has come from national organizations like the Child Welfare League. The Child Welfare League's (June, 1971) board took a position against Title IV of H.R. 1, the "welfare reform" bill, based on the League's "longtime support for a federal guarantee to provide an income floor for all poor families, including the working poor [p. 80]."

The League has long endorsed a national income policy, which it has, at various times, phrased in differing ways.

In 1958, the League (1958) said: "Economic security of families is essential to the welfare of all children [p. 69]."

In 1968, the League (1958) said: "today, despite . . . Social Security benefits and public assistance programs, there still are almost 30 million people, approximately half of whom are children, who live in poverty. We believe the time has come . . . when a floor should be placed under family income. . . . [p. 69]"

In 1971, the League (1971) reiterated its basic position, stating: ". . . we believe that a family income sufficient to meet minimum standards of health and human decency is essential and basic to any program of services for children [p. 80]."

The same League position was reaffirmed in testimony

before the Senate Finance Committee on February 2, 1972.

The fact is that the League (1971), along with a number of other voluntary service organizations and organizations of recipients, knows that income "is essential and basic to any program of services [p. 80]"—whether for children or families. Until the basic, fundamental, essential principle of an income guarantee is accepted, [we realize] the services provided will be relatively ineffective. It is this need for an income policy that should be at the center of the debate in welfare. It is the matter of "income (or welfare) being a right, not a privilege" that should be debated.

But even those organizations with memberships that consist largely of welfare recipients or poor people who are opposing the "welfare reform" bill might hesitate to endorse the logical program that grows out of the recognition that "welfare is a right, not a privilege." The guidelines for such a national welfare plan might be:

1. Make welfare a service, not a profit-making business;
2. Pay for all welfare services with a progressive tax on total wealth—personal and corporate;
3. Administer welfare programs locally through representatives of recipients and welfare workers;
4. Provide complete and preventive welfare with no charges for social welfare services.

It is necessary to build a case for a common approach to the provision of all human services precisely because health, education and welfare are so interdependent. Without adequate provision of health, education and welfare as essential human services, none of the three can be effectively provided, no matter how astronomical expenditures may be in any one area. "Fixing up" one, or even two, of the three essential human service systems will not work. Further delay in repairing all three deteriorating services only makes the task more difficult.

The task, at bottom, seems simple enough: provide complete and preventive human services, without charge, to all who need them, under nonprofit auspices, and administer them locally through representatives of service receivers and service-givers. Pay for all human services with a progressive tax on total wealth. Create federal nonprofit corporations to produce and distribute such materials and supplies as are required to allow the human service systems to function.

That is a recipe for real, major change. Choosing major change, as opposed to the "foot in the door" policy described and endorsed by Daniel Thursz (1972), involves the recognition that the Social Security program has been an inadequate response to the needs of either the aged or the dependent. It is true, as Thursz says, that "Wilbur Cohen and others . . . got their foot in the door . . . and then each year the program was amended until it included more and more people and more and more services [p. 87]."

However, after nearly 40 years of the "foot in the door" approach, the fact is that not enough people are included, not enough services are being provided and those services that are provided are inadequate, and have deteriorated from earlier levels of quality. This is so because throughout the years since the programs were first instituted, most needs have grown geometrically, while services have been provided incrementally, according to the irregular timetable of political happenstance.

Major change, then, is no longer merely the preferable choice over "foot in the door." Because "foot in the door" has failed, major change is the sole choice. Major change sooner simply means that less social and economic dislocation—and attendant human suffering by all concerned—will result later. And, if major change in the human services ecosystem is delayed beyond the point of "critical mass," then our society—just like any environment—is doomed.

Many persons feel that "critical mass" has been

reached, and that the next-to-last step was the nation's blunder into Vietnam. The last step could be enactment of the repressive features of the "welfare reform" bill. The last step could be the failure to adopt an adequate health and nutrition program for all of our citizens. The last step could be the impending destruction of the public schools, that obviously imperfect but critically needed rubber band that binds together the strands of a free and pluralistic society.

The last step could even be something as seemingly insignificant as deciding that day care, like most other human services, must be put through the trial-and-error paces that health services and aged-care have gone through. It may be necessary for ignorant people to repeat their mistakes. It ought not be necessary when it will be children—especially poor children—who will have to pay for such mistakes, merely because it takes courage to put an end to the human experimentation now. Children are one of our last "resources"—do they have to be "strip mined" too because we are too timid?

Other "resources" have been exploited. Some were material—like the land and the water and the air that we will be paying to restore for generations to come. Some were human—the aged, who have already died; the parents, who have already lost their chance for decent health, for decent education and who will probably die in dismal poverty; and the children, who are being destroyed in an effective (if inadvertent) process of race-and-class extermination.

A lot of exploitation involves self-seeking "profiting." But substantial suffering takes place as a result of a kind of self-seeking, a kind of self-profiting that exists in *both* the private sector and the voluntary sector.

In the voluntary sector, the self-seeking and "profiting" is so subtle that it escapes notice—at least in the voluntary sector. An example of such self-seeking is the "foot in the door" approach. Thursz (1972), who seems to endorse the incremental approach, cites the sort of "profiting" I speak of. He tells us that, "In 1962, social workers testified before congressional committees that poverty could be reduced substantially if caseloads for public welfare employees were made smaller [p. 86]." Thursz goes on to say that ". . . to argue that this would have a significant impact on the number of poor people was ridiculous [p. 86]." Thursz says it is ". . . invalid to suggest that social workers did not want a program of guaranteed income because they might lose their jobs [p. 87]." But instead of concluding that "social services are essential, but income protection is even more essential," Thursz backs away. He takes the poition that we have heard almost every segment of society take: I'm for change so long as my status remains relatively stable. In his own words:

> Income protection is essential, but social services are also essential. Let us not support those who speak of saving money by dissassembling the network of social services and using these funds to provide income protection [p. 87].

We have heard similar words from others. The union leader says, "Equal employment opportunity is essential, but job seniority is also essential." The business executive says, "Preserving our environment is essential, but low-cost production of goods is also essential." The legislator says, "Doing what is right is essential, but getting elected is also essential."

At a certain point—whether one is a social worker, a union leader, a business executive or a legislator—it is necessary to take the hard step of sacrificing one's own best short-term interests for the sake of society's more important long-term interests.

All of this bears very directly on the large issue of whether it is right to profit from any human service and, more specifically, whether it is right to profit from day care.

Day care is no different from health services, from education, from the other child welfare services. The question of profit would never have come up at all if there had not been so many persons—in government, in business and in the voluntary "nonprofit" sector—who were afraid to question one of the primary myths of the free enterprise system; that is the myth that the best product can be bought for the lowest cost through the combination of competition and efficiency which the private, open market guarantees.

"Buying" from private businessmen does not necessarily guarantee that one is purchasing sound, efficient management. Neither the private sector nor the voluntary sector has any magical monopoly on competence. In the private sector, Lockheed, the "profit-making" aerospace company, was not able to design a decent C-5 aircaft and made so little profit that it had to be bailed out by the federal government. The Penn Central railroad bankruptcy is another example.

Big business has a similarly unspectacular record in day care. Several companies are bankrupt or out of business: American Child Centers, Early Achievement Centers and Early Childhood Learning Centers among them. Other day care companies are in deep trouble: Dolphin Clubs' owners are under indictment for grand fraud and Four Seasons is in the process of "reorganization" following a bankruptcy action. Most of the rest are of little consolation to those who would like to find a business with demonstrated capability in the day care field. Little Shavers is little involved in day care centers at all any more. Romper Room is still the name of the television show and not a thriving chain. Universal Education Corporation's contract with the State of Pennsylvania for day care has been labeled a "boondoggle" by the *Harrisburg* (Pa.) *Patroit.*

As most of those who had ever been involved with day care knew, and as most of the investment community has learned, businessmen cannot on an "open market" basis make a reasonable profit from day care and offer a quality service at the same time. All other things being equal, it simply costs more, or one must deliver less, if one offers the same thing at the same price as a competitor who need not show a profit.

Serious questions about whether day care could turn a profit would never have been raised at all, if those with the responsibility to provide day care, seen as part of a larger public responsibility for human services, had had an opportunity to do their job. But these people, who were, by and large, in the voluntary sector, had their hands full trying to keep other, larger human service systems from disintegrating altogether.

The situation was very similar to the one that faced voluntary providers of care for the aged prior to the enactment of Medicare-Medicaid. They were underfinanced, underorganized and threatened with the spectre of being "un-American" if they suggested that health for the aged, like education for the young, was a "public responsibility." The health care "establishment" at the time felt that the private, fee-based system was somehow intrinsic to the quality of health care.

However, since then, our experience with the care for the aged since the enactment of Medicare and Medicaid has provoked a giant step toward demythologizing the image of business as the efficient deliverer of human services.

When the prospect of massive federal spending for nursing home care arose in the early days of Medicare and Medicaid, big business moved quickly and formed a powerful lobby focused on getting federal funds for proprietary (e.g., private) nursing homes. The voluntary forces—largely under religious auspices—who had been historically responsible for the lion's share of services to the aged, were legally barred from intensive lobbying activities, and therefore were left out of much of the legislation that stimulated the spending on—and the growth of—services aimed at the aged. After the federal money started flowing and the proprietary nursing home lobby did its effective work, the historical situation was reversed. Now 90 percent of the nursing home services, mostly funded by public money, are under the control of the profit-makers. During the last few years, shares of the "nursing home chains" have become "glamor stocks."

One of the most powerful organizations to comment on the outcome of the nursing home situation is the AFL-CIO (1971). Citing ". . . atrocious cruelties and abuses of public and private funds [that] cry out for correction," the AFL-CIO has called on the Administration and the Congress to take the following remedial action as the number one step:

> Encourage nonprofit institutions providing nursing-home care by including them in all programs, gradually phasing out public financing of institutions motivated by profit. [p. 3].

At this point, the health businessmen have been discredited to the extent that John H. Knowles, M.D., (undated) president of the Rockefeller Foundation, can say:

> . . . medical care in this country is . . . a private business operating for the convenience of the practioner—and not the needs of the sick. . . .

What possible set of circumstances, save the profiteering by those businessmen who got in on the Medicare-Medicaid-inspired health care gold rush, could have led Senator Long, the politically and fiscally conservative chairman of the Senate Finance Committee, to suggest a new way to handle the massive new day care money included in the "welfare reform" bill? Perhaps the prospect that the same speculators who had engineered the "chain" nursing home boom were gearing up to divert a healthy portion of the new day care money was too much; maybe that is the real reason behind the Federal Child Care Corporation.

Predictably, the smell of federal money has brought the day care businessmen together in a lobby. A national organization of owners of private day care centers was established in Chicago during 1971. The group, which is called the National Association for Child Development and Education, was reportedly *(Chicago Sun-Times,* p. 45) organized by 14 persons from around the country representing 244 private centers.

But this time the human services entrepreneurs are working at a slight disadvantage. Forces as seemingly opposed as Senator Long and the Medical Committee for Human Rights agree on one key concept: if you are passing out the taxpayers money to purchase services, you stand to get cheated less by the vendors if you have a federal non-profit corporation in charge.

And other groups and individuals are determined that children in day care will escape the strip mining, rake-off process that the aged had to endure—contradicting, thereby, the position of President Nixon (1971), who has said that,

> the Federal Government's role wherever possible should be one of assisting parents to purchase needed day care services in the private, open market . . . [p. 521130].

As with every other service, day care, in the mind of President Nixon and many other people, is no different than any other commodity traded according to the laws of supply and demand: sell at the lowest possible price and—to use the term made familiar by the Pentagon—keep "cost-benefit" ratios in mind.

Immense pressure will be generated by businessmen seeking profits through new day care programs. But an impressive counterforce is determined that the mistakes made with nursing homes, where the "private, open market" proved to be such a disservice to the aged, shall not be repeated.

Certainly the Child Development Coalition, the group of organizations that recently drew up a list of legislative recommendations to be incorporated in any new comprehensive child development legislation introduced this year have made this clear. That group, which includes such organizations as the AFL-CIO, Common Cause, the Leadership Conference on Civil Rights, the League of Women Voters, the National Council of Churches, the National Education Association, the National Urban Coalition, the National Urban League, the National Welfare Rights Organization, the United Auto Workers and the United Steelworkers of America, has called, in a memo to its membership, for the following:

> ... an absolute prohibition against profit-making child care programs, with changes of all references in the bill from "public or private agency (or agencies)" to "public or private nonprofit agency (or agencies [January 28, 1972]."

In addition, a recent meeting convened as the National Child Development Action Conference (1972) under the auspices of the Day Care and Child Development Council of America, which had 1,200 participants, passed a similar resolution:

> ... the federal government must appropriate adequate funds for private nonprofit and public quality day care and child development programs [p. 6].

Other organizations, such as the American Federation of Teachers (AFL-CIO), have already set quality standards which call (Stern, 1971) for programs to be operated under nonprofit, public-school auspices.

And the 1972 report (Keyserling, 1972) of the National Council of Jewish Women, compiled from 77 selected reports from 90 cooperating local Sections, gives additional evidence in favor of nonprofit program operations. The report, entitled "Windows on Day Care," found that:

> ... Only one percent of the proprietary centers visited were considered "superior," 15 percent were regarded as "good." An additional thirty-five percent were essen-

tially custodial, providing "fair" care in the sense of meeting basic physical needs with very little, if any, by way of developmental services. Half were considered to be rendering poor care and in some cases this was found to be very bad indeed [p. 4].

There are very different findings for nonprofit centers:

. . . Of all nonprofit centers seen, nearly a tenth were regarded as "superior," providing care as good as any found. Somewhat more than were considered "good," and about half were rated "fair," meaning that while they provided for basic physical needs they were essentially custodial. Somewhat more than a tenth were considered "poor" [pp. 4-5].

Rearranged in tabular form, the comparison between proprietary and nonprofit centers would be:

superior—1 percent of proprietary centers, 10 percent of nonprofit centers;
good—15 percent of proprietary centers, 25 percent of non-profit centers;
fair—35 percent of proprietary centers, 50 percent of non-profit centers;

And in the critical "poor" category? 50 percent of the proprietary centers were giving poor care compared to somewhat more than 10 percent of the nonprofit centers.

Neither proprietary nor nonprofit centers are doing what they should, but nonprofit centers are clearly doing the better job for children.

Not even the squabbling among the interdisciplinary forces that claim jurisdiction over day care is likely to let them forget the history of commercialized health care, the power of a lobby financed by businessmen anxious to profit from human services or the record of performance that exists that rules out proprietary day care.

The real threat and the real battle over day care is not between the Office of Education and its allies, teachers, or between the Community Services Administration of Social and Rehabilitation Services and the social workers, or between the Office of Child Development and the psychologists or between the other forces vying for bureaucratic control at this time. Any one of these forces—or some other set of agency and professional allies—could win the battle for control of day care and lose the future of America's children.

Unfortunately, the very controversy over the day care issue did distract people from H.R. 1 and its basic issue, adequate income. Activity aimed at passing the child development bill as part of 1971's Economic Opportunity Act extension diverted attention from much more serious Congressional activity affecting children and families. The media were full of charges and countercharges over the child development provisions, and progressive politicians of all stripes were posturing for the public. All sorts of groups lost sight of the principle in the fight over one bill. But while all the grandstanding was taking place over a questionable, minor piece of legislation, amendments to the Social Security Act which tightened the screws on welfare recipients slithered through Congress.

The failure of the more progressive body, the Senate, to stop the move against welfare recipients is being repeated: Note the liberal, progressive Senators who are in favor of day care or child development legislation, most of which is even less acceptable than the thoroughly compromised version President Nixon vetoed. The list includes the very sort of Senators that one would expect to find fighting for the principle of adequate income and against Title IV of the "welfare reform" bill. With a few exceptions, the strongest advocates of a child care bill are co-sponsors of a set of "liberalized," but still inadequate, amendments to the "welfare reform" bill. Such Senators are, in effect, working to grant children a nickel's worth of benefits through a child care bill. Inadvertently, those same Senators, in working for President Nixon's "welfare" bill, were about to take away the dollar's worth of benefits children and their families then had.

There is hope, however, that the legislative situation which is now so confusing even to experienced, liberal and progressive members of the Senate will be clarified before the mistakes of 1967 are repeated again. In 1967, as now, well-meaning Senators worked for "liberalizing" amendments to a bad welfare bill, only to see them discarded in the Senate-House conference on the bill.

If, as seems likely, the Congress wishes to pass legislation which will improve child care in this nation, the basic step should be to pass legislation providing for an adequate income for all citizens. But such legislation cannot pass at this point; instead, repressive legislation, mislabeled and sold as a bill providing a floor under income, has already passed the House.

Decent legislation to provide child care is needed, but such legislation should meet requirements like those recommended by the Child Welfare League (September, 1971). An empty bill, that faces little prospect for appropriations, that is largely concerned with which set of government-sponsored politicians, bureaucrats and professionals will be in control, and which leaves the field wide open to the proprietary day care businessmen, is not worth battling over.

The real struggle taking place at this time behind the smokescreen of the various "child development" bills, as Gilbert Steiner (1972) notes in his recent article "Child Care: New Social Policy Battleground," is whether or not programs for children will be financed within an overall scheme of human services, featuring shared control between service-receivers and service-givers.

Steiner, who believes that most day care programs

should be included as part of the general idea of public
responsibility for children that has been behind public support of the public school system, says:

> An extension of the publicly financed school system to
> envelop children younger than those the system tradi-
> tionally has served and to provide health and nutrition
> services not provided by many schools is the heart of the
> policy issue. Because behavioral research has shown the
> importance of early education in child development,
> the consequences of extensive federal involvement in
> such a policy are both supported and feared. Parental
> control is proposed as a way of guarding against gov-
> ernment regimentation while making use of federal
> money. But organized parental control of an educa-
> tional apparatus could evolve into a new kind of com-
> munity action agency. Rather than renew the problems
> created by community action in the past, state and local
> officials would prefer to assume policy control of com-
> prehensive child-care programs themselves.
>
> This conflict between government and communi-
> ty forces is unsettled. So is the fundamental philosophi-
> cal conflict between child care as a program for the
> poor and child development as a public investment
> [pp. 8-9].

In welfare and in day care, an acceptance of new kinds
of relationships and immense effort are going to be necessary. The nation must come to realize that "day care is a
right, not a privilege," and that such a national position on
day care is part of the overriding, basic understanding that
"human services are a right, not a privilege."

REFERENCES

AFL-CIO Executive Council on Nursing Homes. State-
    ment of February 16, 1971.
Chicago Sun-Times. National day care owners' group set up.
    February 29, 1972: 45.

Child Welfare League of America. Statement prepared for Senate Finance Committee Hearing. In *Child care, hearings.* September 22-24, 1971, pp. 479-480.

Child Welfare League of America. Position statement on Title IV, Family Programs, of H.R. 1. June 17, 1971.

Child Welfare League of America. Position statement on income policy. December 5, 1968.

Chisholm, S. Open letter on behalf of the Medical Committee for Human Rights. March 15, 1972.

Conner, E. & Ellena, J. The realities of school finance. Washington, D.C.: American Association of School Administrators, undated.

Harrisburg Patriot (Pa.). Editorial, April 26, 1971.

Keyserling, M. *Windows on day care.* New York: National Council of Jewish Women, 1972.

Knowles, H. H. As cited in Medical Committee for Human Rights, *MCHR is.* Chicago: MCHR, undated.

Medical Committee for Human Rights. *MCHR is.* Chicago: MCHR, undated.

National Child Development Action Conference. Resolutions passed in plenary session. *Voice for Children,* March 1972, **5** (3).

Nixon, R. Economic opportunity amendments of 1971 veto message (H.Doc. No. 92 48). *Congressional Record,* December 10, 1971.

Royster, Me-tooism? *Wall Street Journal,* January 19, 1972: 10.

Steiner, G. Y. Child care: new social policy battleground. *The Brookings Bulletin.* Winter 1972, **9** (1): 6-9.

Stern, California children's centers. *American Teacher.* December 1971: 16.

Thursz, Can we insure a bright future for our children? *Child Welfare,* 1972, **LI,** (2); 87.

Titmuss, R. *The gift relationship: from human blood to social policy.* New York: Pantheon, 1971.

Washington Evening Star. (Washington, D.C.) Rep. Green encouraged. March 17, 1972, Section E: 4.

Chapter Eight

HOW TO PLAN
FOR A COMPREHENSIVE
DAY CARE SYSTEM

Glen P. Nimnicht

Instead of attempting to predict what day care may become in the United States, I want instead to combine some pragmatic considerations with some idealism. The result, of course, will be less than the idealist might hope for and more than most practical people will see as possible.

First, we must place day care into some context of a general program for the healthy development of all young children. No one could reasonably expect in the foreseeable future that any combination of federal, state and local governments, industry and profit-making day care services could provide quality day care for all of the children in the United States at a cost that people could afford. Furthermore, no evidence exists that this would be desirable, even if it were possible. Day care should be one of many alternatives for the care of young children.

Obviously, if one of the objectives of an early childhood development program is to strengthen the parents' capacity as parents, those parents who want to care for their own children should be helped to do so as a fundamental aspect of the program. In explicit terms, this means that if a parent prefers to stay at home and care for the children instead of working, he or she should have adequate support to remain at home. In addition, if the parent is interested in learning more about child development and how to care for the child, the training should be available.

A second alternative is half-day programs for those parents who want to have the major responsibility for the development and nurturing of their children, but who desire some outside child care either for the development of the child or to allow some time to pursue other activities.

The third alternative, of course, is full-time day care services for those parents who prefer to be free to work or pursue other activities.

Given the temperament of the parents, any one of these three alternatives would strengthen their capacity to be effective as parents. But it seems obvious to me that for those parents who have the interest and the temperament to care for young children, the best way to serve them and their children is to provide the support and services necessary to help them stay at home. There is no indication of any kind that we need additional persons in the labor force; in fact, all of the current indicators are to the contrary. Thus, the policy of providing day care services to push the low-income parent into taking a job or entering a training program that may or may not lead to a job is not a sound policy. The parent, the child and the economy would be better off if the parent stayed at home. In fact, even the short-term economic benefits raise questions. The idea that day care services will save money by reducing the welfare rolls by enabling the parents to leave the home and take a job is certainly questionable. For children who are not old enough to attend public schools, a quality day care program costs $2,000 per child. Even when a parent has only two children who would require day care service, the economy of paying for day care rather than welfare does not stand under scrutiny.

Affirmation of the traditional American work ethic strongly motivates the clamor for reducing welfare roles.

This movement, however, often overlooks the fact that care of one's own children has traditionally been considered, in our society a legitimate occupation.

Following this line of reasoning, the justification for day care programs is to provide quality programs for those parents who currently need day care services and those parents who want such services. To me, this justification suffices. The exorbitant claims made about the benefits or needs of day care do not bring the necessary services any closer.

The model that follows is one example of the way that day care can fit into a broader, more comprehensive system of child development:

The model is based upon the use of a Head Start or similar program as the hub of the system. A comprehensive Head Start program provides three-, four-, and five-year-old children with a classroom experience designed to promote their physical, social, emotional and intellectual development. Furthermore, an effective Head Start program provides social, psychological and health services for both the children and parents. Such a program could be strengthened to provide additional services for the training of day care mothers, a central materials library for the day care homes and parent education programs to improve the parents ability to attend to their own children.

Such a program would present parents with three alternatives based upon their needs and desires.

The first alternative would provide the least amount of service, but would do the most to develop the parents' independence and capacity to attend to their children. The center would provide such necessary support services as health care and offer the parents training to improve their skills in nurturing the development of their own children. Such training programs already exist; one example is the Parent/Child Toy-Lending Library developed under my direction at the Far West Laboratory in San Francisco, California.

In the Toy-Lending Library program, parents who wish to work at home with their children enroll in an eight-week course in the use of eight educational toys designed to teach specific skills and concepts. During the course, parents meet once a week for two hours to observe demonstrations of the use of the toys, role-play the use of the toys, discuss techniques to help their child develop his or her language ability and develop or maintain a healthy self-concept and discuss topics of school or community concern to the parents. After the course, parents may continue to borrow the eight toys and other games and toys from the Toy-Lending Library.

The second alternative is the conventional half-day Head Start program as it is currently operated.

The third alternative is full-time, day-long day care service. A group of day care homes would be associated with the Head Start center; each day care home would serve up to five children. These day care homes would extend the services of the Head Start center to provide a complete day care service. A working mother would take her child to a neighborhood day care home, and the operator of the home would bring the children to the Head Start center for three hours each day. During that time she could receive training or do her shopping or housework, so that when the children were under her sole care she could fully attend to their needs.

We use this simple model to illustrate many of our concerns about day care in the future. First, the model is based upon an operational program that is funded by the government—either federal or state. Industry-supported day care does not play a role in it nor does day care service for a profit fit into the scheme. Both omissions are intentional on my part.

I view industry's current interest in supporting day care as a worthwhile but transitional step in the development of day care services. It is worthwhile because it helps to generate interest in day care and to build the public support that is essential for government-supported day care operations. I predict that some of the strongest support of government-sponsored programs will come from industries that have tried to operate their own programs. Those industries are discovering that day care is expensive and complicated. The notion of locating the day care center at the plant where the parent works is very appealing until it is tried. Theoretically, the parent can bring the child upon arriving at work and take the child home upon leaving. Parents can have lunch with the children and perhaps spend one day a month working in the center. In reality, some parents spend an hour each way travelling to and from work. This schedule comprises an eleven or twelve hour day for the child; hence that hour on the way home in the car or on a bus is not a pleasant experience for either the child or the parent. Furthermore, the parents often do a little shopping after work before they pick up the child or they work a little overtime; thus the 8:00 A.M. to 5:30 P.M. schedule that was planned for the center often becomes an 8:00 A.M. to 6:30 P.M. schedule. The idea of the parents having lunch with the child is a good one, but the schedules do not always mesh, and eating in the center or taking the child to the cafeteria may be less pleasant than expected. The idea that the parents might work one day a month in the center is also a good one, but it overlooks the fact that many parents work because they do not like to care for young children. Supervisors may resist their employees' missing a day's work, and employees may return to the job to find a day's backlog of work awaiting them. Probably of more concern to the management is the gradual discovery that a new variable in personnel management is introduced by having the day care center at the plant. Whose children gain acceptance to the center? How much does the employer have to pay? What about those employees who do not benefit from the service? A subtle but important change in the management of the center may also occur. Suppose, for example, that the president's secretary has a child in the center. She is unhappy about something that has happened and discusses it with the president. He responds with a memo asking what the problem is that goes down the chain of command. A new dimension has been added to the system.

If the center is located where most of the workers live, instead of at the plant, some of those problems are avoided. However, most likely only a few employees will live in a location that will conveniently allow them to walk with the child to the center or drop him off on the way to work. Depending on the distance from the plant to the center, the hours the center must be open are extended and the work day for the employee is longer. The company may find that on the basis of a survey of employees it planned and staffed a center for 100 children, but that it has ended up with only 50. What started out as a rather expensive proposition is now extremely costly. Thus, I suspect that some of the strongest support for government-operated and supported day care will come from persons with experience in industrial programs.

Even if this does not result and even if the industrial center works better than current experience indicates, I have serious reservations about such centers. One of the major arguments for industry-supported day care is that it should reduce absenteeism and turnover. If turnover could be sharply reduced, the saving that would result from not having to continually train new people for entrance level positions would offset much of the cost of the day care program. The logic is sound but we do not yet know if it holds up in practice. Furthermore, to the extent that it does hold up, it has a negative as well as positive aspect. For the employer, industry-provided day care may reduce turnover. For the employee, it provides quality care for his or her child during working hours, but it may also lock the parent into a job that he or she can only leave at the cost of losing the day care service provided by the company.

I deliberately omitted profit-making day care from this model because it does not seem practical. First, evidence suggests that private groups can operate day care centers at a profit only by incurring higher costs than government-operated centers. As in any other educational program, the bulk of the expense in operating day care programs is personnel cost. There are only three ways of reducing personnel cost: (1) paying less for services; (2) increasing the number of children served by each adult; or (3) reducing services such as health care. A reasonable and legitimate way to reduce personnel cost is the cooperative nursery approach in which parents "pay" part of the fee by working in the center, but this offers no solution to the working parent. The other method of paying less for personnel means that some staff members may be exploited and kept in poverty or on the borderline of poverty.

Reducing the proportion of adults per child can be accomplished only by reducing the quality of the program. A reduction of other services, such as health care, is justified if the family has access to the services elsewhere or can afford to pay for them.

I do not mean to imply that I oppose private profit-making day care centers, since some people can and are willing to pay for such services, but the centers do not provide a basis for a comprehensive day care program. The concept of efficient, economical, national distribution of day care in a manner similar to the distribution of fried chicken does not square with the realities of day care. Such a notion also runs counter to the idea of local control of the center and parent participation in the decisions that affect the operation of the centers. At their best, Head Start programs are good models of local control of a nationally funded program.

The effects of large institutionalized day care centers

on young children also concern me. Edward Zigler, former director of the Office of Child Development and now of Yale University has observed that

> When we think of child care, the image that typically comes to mind is our conventional center with from 12 to 20 children. What is often overlooked is that the bulk of children who are presently in day care are in family day care homes which typically serve four, six or eight children.

He could have gone on to say that as of 1969, only six percent of the children of working mothers were cared for in group day care centers (White House Conference on Children, 1970).

The fact that 94 percent of the children receive day care services outside centers leaves no doubt about the importance of focusing attention on this area, but two different approaches could be taken. The first would be to attempt to transfer day care services to centers and terminate day care homes; the second would be to strengthen the homes. The model I have outlined takes the second alternative because I believe that if day care homes or small centers can offer quality comprehensive services, they are more desirable as day care situations than are large centers.

In order to offer quality comprehensive services, day care homes and small neighborhood centers need the following:

—A training program to help the operators increase their competency, particularly in the area of an educational component in the program;
—Support services such as health, nutritional and social services;
—Back-up assistance to provide adequate care for children when the day care mother is ill or has other problems;
—Parent education and involvement programs;

—A support center for children whose parents work unusual hours and for emergency care of children;

—A source of educational materials that can be used on a rotating basis to provide a stimulating environment;

—Supervision to make certain that the day care home maintains a quality program.

The model that was outlined earlier can satisfy those conditions. There are two reasons for recommending that we focus attention on day care homes and small centers. The first is pragmatic. As Zigler points out, most of the children are currently receiving day care in homes, and without any kind of massive federal support. Most of the children will continue to receive care in homes for some time to come. The problem of locating adequate facilities that meet fire and safety standards for moderate to large day care centers will take time to solve. Thus the greatest good for the largest number of children will come from improving day care in licensed day care homes and non-licensed homes.

The social and educational advantages comprise the second reason I advocate strengthening the day care home. Chapman and Lazar (1971, p. 14) report that centers of moderate size, between 30 and 60 children, tend to be of highest quality. But they also report: (1) that day care homes are better than many professionals believe (p. 34); and, (2) that nearly all researchers who have written on the subject comment on the advantages of family day care systems, i.e., warm and responsible care, better ability to service children with special problems, the fact that the child remains in his neighborhood, age-mix, and the fact that the day care mother is often better educated than day care center staff (p. 33).

The limitation, they point out, is that home day care programs tend to have few or no educational components (p. 13). A small research project that has just been completed by the Laboratory reinforces this statement (Addison, 1972). The project evaluated a ten-week training program in Richmond, California that was based upon the use of toys and games to improve the educational component of services of day care mothers. The project was carried out in cooperation with the Richmond Model Cities Program and Contra Costa Junior College. The six day care mothers who had expressed the greatest interest were selected for training by the Model Cities day care director. Addison visited the homes before the class started and interviewed the mothers. None of the homes contained materials that indicated a concern for the intellectual development of children and the mothers did not really understand the concept of an educational component. At the end of the ten weeks, all of the mothers were using the educational toys and demonstrated through other signs, such as displaying childrens' work on the walls, that they had become aware of the importance of educational development. Addison concluded that all of the mothers now recognized the need to do more to help children develop their intellectual ability, but that the mothers needed more than the ten-week course to develop an understanding of what they could do and insure a continued interest on their part. This study reinforces the notion that day care operators need training to provide quality service and that they benefit from even a limited amount of training over a short period of time.

In this context, it is interesting to note that the qualifications of the staff *per se* are not related to a quality program (Chapman & Lazar, 1971, p. 37), but that training is obviously necessary. Since the survey tends to agree that day care home operators are more child oriented (p. 34) and provide warm, responsible care, a self-selection factor seems to be at work. If this is true, providing training to increase the operator's skills is a fairly easy task because it is not necessary to change attitudes.

Chapman and Lazar (p. 13) concluded that moderate size centers serving from 30 to 60 children were of higher quality than smaller or larger centers. They also point out that as size increases centers become sterile, administrative complexity increases, and the environment becomes more impersonal. Although they were referring to centers with 60 or more children, I believe that the same problems apply to smaller centers. From my own experience in operating a nursery school for 30 children, from the Laboratory's experience with a day care center for 50 children and from conversations with others in the field, I have made the following observations:

—Administrative and logistical problems are related to size. For example, unless the center is in a densely populated area, transportation becomes a problem in a center for 25 to 30 children;

—Dealing with five extremely active children in a group of fifty is more difficult than dealing with one such child in a group of ten;

—Children have more difficulty in establishing a sense of belonging and identity in a group of fifty children with several adults with whom to relate, than in a small group with only one or two adults;

—It is more difficult for adults to know individual children in large groups;

—Mass feeding is not as desirable as eating familiar foods in a small group;

Many centers have minimized these problems, but not without an effort. If the same kind of effort went into solving the problems of day care homes, they might provide programs equal in quality to those of the moderate size centers.

A more fundamental question about large centers, however, concerns the long-term effects of placing a young child in an institutional setting for most of his waking hours and keeping him in some institutional environment for the next eighteen years. We do not know the answer and many of the research priorities listed by Office of Child Developmen reflect this concern. It seems certain that large centers are going to be developed before we have an answer, and in many instances there may not be an alternative. In the meantime, however, it seems prudent to strengthen day care homes to provide an alternative where possible.

My final concern about large day care centers relates to their ability to reflect the parents' culture and life style. People seem to forget that day care is not a simple extension of a three-hour program like Head Start. The amount of time for which the child is involved makes a fundamental difference. Head Start supplements the parents' efforts. Day care supplants them; the child is in day care all day every working day of the year. Most of the time the parent has time only to dress the child, take him to a center, pick him up, feed him and put him to bed. Under those circumstances, if I were a Native American I would want my *young* child under the care of another Native American from the same tribal group. Otherwise he is not going to reflect my culture and lifestyle. Furthermore, I would want to reduce the stress on the child by reducing the inconsistencies between the home and the center. The model indicates the best way to cope with such a problem. If the day care home mother is a neighbor from the same ethnic background and with a similar lifestyle, she will reinforce the language and culture of the parents; a small neighborhood Head Start program will provide the child with a broader social experience.

The third concern that I can illustrate with the model is a concern for the participation and involvement of the parents in the education of their children. I think this is important, to strengthen the parents' capacity as parents and to insure that the program responds to the child, his background and his lifestyle. By participation, I mean that parents are actively involving themselves in the education of their children, either by being the major force at home, aided with training and materials, or by working in the center as paid assistants or volunteers or by attending parent education meetings. Obviously the parents who need day care will not be able to participate as fully as others because their time is limited. By involvement, I mean that parents are involved in the decision-making process that affects the education of their children. Obviously every parent cannot be involved in all of the decisions, but a representative group of parents can be involved and can have real power to affect the decisions that determine the operation of the center and day care homes. Through these representatives, the parents can make their decisions known. This concept is implicit in the model I have described.

As I look back at the introduction of this paper, I hope that I am forecasting or predicting to a greater extent than I indicated. Perhaps a self-fulfilling prophecy will be at work and I will see the day when all of the parents who need day care will have it at a price they can afford. It will be recognized that it belongs in the category of social service rather than in the private sector of the economy. It will be a part of a larger system of child care and development that offers parents alternatives and responds to their needs in a sensitive and humanistic way. This is my prophecy—what remains is to make it work.

References

Addison, B. *Evaluation of a training unit in the use of games and toys with day care mothers as part of a college course.* Berkeley, Ca.: Far West Laboratory, (unpublished manuscript), 1972.

Chapman, J.E. & Lazar, J.B. *A review of the present status and future needs in day care research.* Washington, D.C.: Department of Health, Education and Welfare, 1971.

Guide to securing and installing the parent-child toy-lending Library. San Francisco: Far West Laboratory, 1972.

White House Conference on Children. *Profiles on children.* Washington, D.C.: U.S. Government Printing Office, 1970.

Zigler, E. Speech delivered at National Association for the Education of Young Children. Minneapolis, Minn., Nov. 7, 1971.

Chapter Nine

GETTING SUPPORT FOR CHILDREN'S PROGRAMS: ORGANIZING CHILD ADVOCACY

Elizabeth Haas

State and local lobbies on behalf of children are needed for two reasons: First, most of the services and funds for children, youth and families are provided through state and local agencies. Very little will happen unless governors, state legislators and those agencies feel that the public in their state wants action. Secondly, state lobbies are essential to building support for national legislation among senators and congressmen. They respond best to the interests expressed by local constituents. The work of a lobby at the state level is described here.

In every state, groups exist that are concerned with children's programs in their specific areas (for example: mental health, education, juvenile justice, etc.). Their contribution to the continued development of programs for children has been, and will continue to be, invaluable.

The information contained in this article is a first effort to provide information on forming state lobbies. Much of it is based on the successful efforts of the California Children's Lobby. Elizabeth Berger, Executive Director, and Don Fibush, Founder, of the California Children's Lobby, and Jule M. Sugarman, originator of the National Children's Lobby, have been of assistance in its preparation.

However, in only a very few states does a qualified statewide group lobby for the broad interest of all children in their state.

A great deal of interest has been focused on forming children's lobbies at the state level. As national legislation is passed, the state groups have found it necessary to make sure that action is taken at the state level to also pass legislation which implements federal authorizations and to make certain that such legislation reflects the best interests of the children it is intended to serve. The need is accentuated by the trend toward revenue sharing, which places decisions on fund usage at state and local levels. State groups, perhaps most importantly, should closely follow their own legislatures to ensure that children get their fair share of budget appropriations, that "good" programs continue to be developed for children and that, where program authority already exists, it is carried out as intended and on a timely basis.

The following material comprises a guide for forming a children's lobby in your state. Where possible, this guide suggests questions and ideas that state groups might consider in organizing their lobbies. These are merely suggestions and are by no means all inclusive. There are many applications on local, county and city levels.

Who Is Interested in a Children's Lobby?

Many more people are interested in a children's lobby than one might think. In every state hundreds of persons lobby personally for children. They all have one characteristic in common, that they care about their own children and other children. But there are also many differences among these people. Some of them care most about one particular kind of problem, while others are concerned with total needs. Some are affiliated with organizations; others operate as individuals. Some are visible and vocal;

others work quietly behind the scenes. Some have money to help; others have only their own time and skill. Some are highly educated; others have only limited training. Some are easy to work with; others are a pain. *The point is that a state lobby needs to reach them all, for strength comes only through widespread organization.*

Many different organizations can supply committed potential members to the state lobby:

—Head Start and day care parent organizations;
—Parent-teacher associations;
—Associations for physically handicapped or mentally retarded children;
—Business and professional women's organizations;
—League of Women Voters;
—Church groups;
—Professional groups of pediatricians, dentists, nurses, psychiatrists, psychologists, educators, social workers, nutritionists, home economists, counselors, juvenile court officials and institutional personnel;
—Organizations of foster and adoptive parents;
—Organizations interested in child protection;
—People who operate institutions for children;
—Minority group organizations.

State or local child welfare agencies, the public schools and community action or Model Cities agencies also can provide leads to interested individuals.

Who Can Start a Lobby?

Anyone or any group of individuals with the time and energy can start a lobby. Don't wait to be asked, because the chances are that others are waiting for you to ask them. On the other hand, try to find out very early whether other groups or individuals have already begun making an effort. In addition to checking the sources listed above, you might check with various local newspapers for mention of any other groups.

You may want to begin by organizing only in your own local area and then expanding to other parts of the state. Bear in mind, however, several points:

—Legislators respond best when they feel interest is coming from many parts of the state;
—People in other parts of the state may be reluctant to join an organization that is dominated by a single community;
—Good legislation may need the viewpoints of many types of communities. Specifically, rural, urban and suburban concerns may differ somewhat.

A Word on Picking Leadership

Finding the right leadership presents perhaps the most difficult problem in organizing a lobby. Chances are that no individual will have all the characteristics that one might wish. Often, however, a total leadership team can be put together which provides for the lobby's total needs. One very important point—*it really pays to seek out people with different points of view.* Many efforts on behalf of children fail because their leaders know or talk only to people who think just as they do.

Other important leadership criteria include the following:

—Bipartisan involvement is needed;
—Leaders have to have a great deal of time available—probably without pay and sometimes at their own expense (although there may be an organization that will finance their expenses);

—Leaders need to know political leadership or have the initiative and courage to get acquainted;

—Leaders have to be able to work with people of diverse ethnic, racial, economic and social backgrounds;

—Leaders need to have access to the press, radio and TV;

—Leaders have to be in situations where they are free to speak out. This may inhibit public officials or professional organization leaders, but don't lose their participation even if they can't be visible leaders;

—Leaders can be controversial, but not to the point where they may endanger public and legislative conference.

The Organizing Committee—The First Step

An organizing committee, composed; if possible, of people from throughout the state, should be formed to study the feasibility of establishing a state lobby. As soon as this is determined, their next tasks are to:

A. *Recruit funding for the initial phases of organizing.* These include:

—Lawyers fees for drawing up incorporation papers and by laws;

—Incorporation fees;

—Expenses incurred in developing initial public relations pieces used to alert media and to attract membership;

—Miscellaneous expenses: Office supplies, telephone, postage, travel, staff, etc. Try to get as much donated as possible.

B. *Incorporate as a nonprofit organization that is not tax exempt.* In most states a lobbying organization is considered a corporation, and Articles of Incorporation must be filed with the corporation commissioner in the county where the lobby's principal office is located. There is a minimal cost for filing. You must also apply to the state and Internal Revenue Service for nonprofit status.

C. *Open a bank account.* It is easier to open an account after your incorporation papers have been filed, but this is not always necessary. Check with your bank.

D. *Draw up an estimated operating budget for one year.*

E. *Develop bylaws.* The organizing committee, or a smaller steering committee, should draft bylaws for approval of the lobby members. They should include sections on: name of corporation and where it is registered; purpose and goals; membership and meetings; board of directors; officers; reports; examination of books and records; waivers of notice; and amendments.

F. *Select an interim board of directors.*

G. *Set up a business office.*

INTERIM BOARD OF DIRECTORS

The interim board of directors, with the assistance of the organizing committee or steering committee, is responsible for:

A. *Fund raising.* Raising money has never been easy, and the fact that contributions to a lobby are not tax exempt only adds to the difficulties . . . and the challenge. You might want to look into setting up a tax-exempt, nonprofit organization for research and public education to go along with the lobby.

B. *Selecting a nominating committee and preparing criteria for board member nomination.* Be sure to take into account the following groups and factors:

—parents;

—consumers;

—geographic distribution (all parts of the state, rural & urban);

—age;

—sex;

—racial and ethnic balance;

—volunteers and professionals;

—topical diversity (day care, health, child welfare, adoptions, youth, etc.);

—prestige (it is also possible to form a "Friends of the Children's Lobby" group composed of well-known persons who would like to have their names associated with the lobby, but who don't have time for board membership.

Remember, you are setting up an organization to "play politics for our children." Each member of the board must be willing and free to speak out on political issues. Since the lobby is in an early stage of development, it might be wise to leave some seats open so that the board can expand as membership grows. Approval of the members of the board should be by membership vote.

*C. *Determining the policies of the children's lobby.* You need to think out answers to these kinds of questions:

—What does the organization want to do?

—Who can do it?

—Will it be bipartisan or nonpartisan?

—How will it react to events?

—How will it initiate reactions?

—Who is the constituency?

—What will membership fees be?

—Will an organization's vote count the same as an individual member's?

---

*If the board of directors is elected early, these should be some of their first actions. If not, these decisions should be approved by the interim board.

1. *Establishing the criteria for determining priorities.*
   —Does it affect large numbers of children?
   —Is it preventive rather than remedial?
   —Does it have long-range impact on children?
   —Are large amounts of money already being spent in the general area?
   —Does it affect younger children?
   —Does it have the interest of your board members? Membership? General public?
   —Does it have some support among legislators? Professionals? Volunteer associations?
   —Do you have the money? Manpower? Time? Expertise?
   —What are possibilities of success?
   —What is public relations potential?
   —What is long-range impact on membership?
   —Who will your enemies be?
   —Does the issue affect people in all economic strata?
   —Is this covered by other interest groups?
2. *Establishing the criteria for designing strategy.*
   —What does the governor think about the issue? Is there somebody on his staff who can be helpful?
   —Will the effort require changes in regulations of agencies?
   —Will the effort require changes in legislation? Should you concentrate on committee members? Should you work on all legislators?
   —How will you secure and disseminate information?
   —How will you inaugurate grassroots support?
   —Will this give you the image of an information disseminator?
   —Should you work behind the scenes or in the public eye?

BOARD OF DIRECTORS

Among the duties of the board of directors are:

A. *Fund raising.* This is definitely a recurring theme!

B. *Development or approval of the policies of the lobby.* See Item C above.

C. *Setting up working committees.* Small, tight committees made up of experts and interested individuals with specific assignments seem to work best. Possible committees might include: governmental affairs, finance and nominating, as well as standing committees in special areas like child development, child advocacy, juvenile delinquency, education, child welfare, exceptional children, child abuse and neglect, dangerous toys, child health, physically handicapped, mental retardation, day care, family planning, youth employment, family life, public assistance and welfare reform, marriage and divorce, drug treatment and prevention, etc.

D. *Hiring an executive director.* Look for someone with strong executive and administrative skills, lobbying experience and fund raising knowhow. A lobbyist or a group of lobbyists might be hired separately, leaving the administrative duties, fund raising and public relations to the executive director. Each state has requirements regarding the registration of lobbyists. Check these out carefully. You may need to start with part-time people.

E. *Volunteers.* The Executive Director will find volunteers extremely helpful. They need not only be the "licking and stuffing" variety, but might include public relations people, attorneys, retired legislators and public officials, graduate, college and high school students. Some graduate schools will let their students take Field Placements in conjunction with your lobby.

A Few Ideas on Fund Raising

There are many methods for raising money for the operation of children's lobby business. Among these:

A. *Expand membership.* Dues from members are rarely sufficient by themselves to sustain an organization. It is estimated that it costs $7.50 to process a member (public relations and recruitment) and $4.50 to serve a member (newsletters and other mailings). It is also estimated that if a large mailing brings in a one percent response, it has been successful. However, it is a broad-based, large and active membership that legislators, governors and other public officials listen to and respond to. To expand membership, you might try:

—Bulk mailings of a brochure or a "What is the Children's Lobby" letter. Try to get lists of PTA's, members of agencies and organizations in specialized children's areas (day care centers, parents organizations, women's lib groups, foster care agencies, pediatricians, etc.), board members of child-oriented organizations (Aid to Retarded Children, Social Planning Councils, etc.). It is possible to bill a member through his Bank Americard or Master Charge card;

—"Chain letters." Ask each member either to recruit 10 new members or to send you the names and addresses of 10 prospective members;

—County meetings. Try to get someone from each county to arrange a meeting with a speaker (legislator, someone known in the community as a child advocate, etc.) or an informal get-together to recruit more members or potential large contributors;

—Professional fund raiser. If you cannot afford to hire the services of a professional fund raiser, it

might be possible to obtain limited consultation;
—Media. Radio, television, newspapers, magazines and professional journals should be approached. Always include your lobby's address and phone number.

B. *Benefits and other ideas on fund raising.*
—Performances. Performers in your area who are widely known or who are known as children's performers might agree to put on a family benefit concert;
—"Walk for Children." Set out a 25-mile course through town. Ask high school students to agree to join your "Walk for Children." They get patrons to pledge a certain amount for each mile of the course walked;
—Holiday cards or stationery. Cards designed by children can be sold with the profits going to the children's lobby. Be sure to check state and local tax requirements and whether you can get an exemption.

A lobby of interested persons working for children at the local, county, state and federal levels ensures that the highest quality of services will be available to all the families that require child care services. You can assist the programs in your community by becoming involved now in these efforts.

Chapter Ten

WHAT PARENTS WANT FROM DAY CARE

Stevanne Auerbach

During World War II, as millions of women left their homes and families and joined the labor force, the federal government, under the Lanham Act, provided funding for day care centers that served millions of preschool children nationwide. Day care, begun in a time of national crisis and inextricably associated in the public mind with the extraordinary circumstances that produced it, fell dormant with the end of the war and the termination of Lanham Act funding. The nation reverted to its traditional assumption that the responsibility for child rearing lay with the mother in her own home, and that the energies of social agencies and the government should again direct themselves toward preserving that relationship between a mother and her children.

In recent years, however, many new social developments have challenged traditional assumptions regarding family life and child rearing. Society's heightened appreciation for the contributions women can make outside and beyond the role of homemaker-mother, the proliferation and greater public acceptance of single mothers and the general economic squeeze have drawn millions of mothers into the labor force (Auerbach, 1972; Bronfenbrenner, 1972). In 1940, one mother in eight worked. By 1960, this figure had increased to one in three, and in 1970 it stood at more than half.

Additional factors encouraging the increase in the number of working mothers include a shift in basic industrial systems toward a higher percentage of white collar jobs; the earlier completion of smaller families, freeing younger women to seek employment; and a great reduction of household drudgery through a vast array of household appliances and labor-saving devices.

The resurgence of interest in day care is not, however, entirely due to the swelling ranks of working mothers. Behavioral research has emphasized that if a child is eventually to attain the fullest development of his social and intellectual potential, early exposure to developmental education opportunities is of prime importance.

As a result, the demand for quality child care has arisen from many quarters; from educated and highly trained women seeking professional fulfillment, from single mothers struggling to achieve or maintain financial independence, from women who would rather work than resign themselves to a meager and frustrating welfare dependency and from women who simply want to contribute to their own and their families' economic well-being (Frost, 1973).

The availability of places in day care programs has not kept pace with demand, however, and many mothers find their return to the labor force either frustratingly hindered or blocked altogether. Many other mothers find themselves involved with day care situations that are either woefully lacking in quality, grossly inconvenient to their daily schedules, prohibitively expensive, or at considerable variance to their personal philosophies of child rearing. These shortcomings are not inherent to the concept of day care, for often a successful program enjoying the enthusiastic support of its staff and parents shines through the general fog of disappointment and disillusionment.

In 1972, I began a personal, informal investigation of the day care situation in San Francisco, talking with scores of parents, day care providers, city, state and federal legislators and administrators. I soon recognized that the greatest obstacle to expanded and improved day care programs lay in the poor communication among parents, between parents and social agencies and among various social and government agencies. Ignorance, or perhaps worse, misunderstanding based on misinformation, abounded.

I decided to undertake a project which would make a concrete and sorely needed contribution toward improving communication among persons committed to providing quality day care programs.

My greatest concern lay with the group who struggled the most and stood to gain the most from day care, mothers and their families. From my extensive contacts with working mothers, I began to see a pattern emerge from the common hopes, expectations, frustrations and problems they expressed. Some of the sentiments they voiced were nearly universal. Others were more individual and personal, but no less compelling. Some mothers had never before been asked for their opinions; others had had their views fall on seemingly deaf ears. Through a systematic survey and interviews with a carefully selected cross section of working mothers of different ethnic and socioeconomic groups involved in the full range of child care programs in San Francisco, I sought to bring into sharper focus the relative priorities that mothers expected and desired from day care programs and to present a clearly defined picture of the sources of their most common praises and complaints.

The theme that underlay all the interviews with mothers was that they most need the assurance that the centers care about them and their children as human beings; and so strong is this need, that it almost doesn't matter what the program contains. Their highest priorities concerned aspects of the "custodial" component of the center programs, e.g., what mothers relate to most directly from their own experiences in caring for their children. They want a safe, bright, cheerful place with a loving, knowledgeable staff willing and able to give their children individual attention. They want day care providers who understand the difficulties mothers face in managing their everyday lives and who will account for these difficulties in their dealings with mothers.

In addition to the day care programs themselves, the mothers frequently cited problems and disappointments having to do with other aspects of day care. Nine out of ten mothers had overwhelming problems finding day care arrangements. After an average of eight months on a waiting list, they then had difficulties getting their children to the centers and themselves to work. They lacked time to attend meetings. Their ability to hold a job was threatened if they had to take time off to be with a sick child. Since day care was usually essential if the mothers were to be able to organize and manage their lives, they expected that it would more nearly accommodate their requirements regarding scheduling, transportation and the fact that they needed freedom to work with a minimum of interruption. They need day care operators who show compassion and genuine interest in their children and, in the case of the foreign-born, they need operators who speak their language. Mothers so infrequently find relief from these functional problems and distractions that they have little time or information with which to evaluate program content. They seek assurances that the day care operators are professionally qualified to deal with educational questions.

Many mothers must first overcome a formidable psychological barrier before they can comfortably consider placing their children in day care programs. Traditional, romanticized attitudes toward motherhood have stressed the idea that mothers have a responsibility to stay home with their young children to ensure that the children receive affection and attention. As recently as 1971, former President Nixon vetoed major child care legislation, citing it as a threat to the sanctity and stability of the American family.

Ideally, the day care center should work in close partnership with the family to supplement, and not substitute for, the unique bond between mother and child. The noted child expert, Urie Bronfenbrenner, offers a definition of a mutually beneficial relationship between the day care center and the home:

> A primary objective of day care and child development programs is to provide a service for families. This objective negates the idea that these programs should replace the rights and responsibilities that are inherently those of the parent. Therefore, an underlying principle for effective day care programming is policy control, program implementation and operation by consumers of the service. This control may be exercised by all of the consumers, or at least by a majority of them. [Bronfenbrenner, 1972].

Another view of the essential role for parents is stated by Robert Hess:

> If we are to continue to value the "uniqueness" of each child, it seems even more important to have the Day Care staff work closely with the parents so that extra-familial care can incorporate some of the individuality of each parent-child pair [Hess, 1972].

Despite the desire of both parents and day care providers to establish close, trusting and responsive relationships, many impediments stand in the way of attaining this goal.

Mothers typically wait several months on a waiting list before their children gain acceptance to a day care program. Prior to placing their children in a day care program (usually the first one offering an available opening), most mothers deal with the uncertainties of finding and keeping responsible baby sitters. As one mother related:

I interviewed at least a dozen persons before hiring the first sitter. The interviews all took place in the evening when I was exhausted and distracted. The first sitter lasted two weeks, when I decided the bruises on my son's body couldn't have been accidental. For eight months I hired a new sitter almost every three weeks, each time going through the same hassle. One woman kept my son in the crib all day. One never fed him, another changed his diapers only once a day—five minutes before I came home. I was ready to quit working and go on welfare when a place opened up and I was taken off the waiting list at the center.

Mothers complained about the lack of time and energy they could devote to their children. Often the only time they spent with their children occurred early in the morning when both were tired, cranky and rushed, and in the evening, again when both were tired. Preparing dinner and bathing the child were all that many mothers had time for, and many felt varying degrees of guilt as a result. The alternative, welfare, was regarded as even less desirable, for most mothers felt children suffered greater deprivations as their parents struggled to maintain themselves on welfare. Time to participate in the center activities was a rare luxury.

Approximately two out of three mothers are affected by scheduling problems that have to do with getting to work, with the day care centers' hours of operation and with dealing with public transportation. Getting to the center in the morning usually involves rising early, preparing breakfast for the child (since few centers provide breakfast), waiting for and riding buses, often transferring from one to another, hurriedly dropping the child off and catching another bus or two for work.

The cycle repeats itself in the evening, except that mothers, their children, the day care workers and fellow commuters are by then hot, tired and irritable.

As one mother described the situation:

I have to be at work at 8:00. That means I have to get up
at 6:00, feed my daughter, get her and me ready, and
leave by a quarter to seven. We get to the center around
7:20, I drop Nancy off and rush to catch the bus to work.
Usually I make it. I get off at 5:00, and the center closes
at 5:30. A couple of times I was late, and they warned me
that they would have no choice but to give Nancy over to
the police if I wasn't there when they closed. Sometimes
I have to work overtime, and then I have to arrange with
a friend to have Nancy picked up. Sometimes I don't
know if I'll have to stay late until late afternoon, and if I
can't arrange something with a friend and I can't stay
late, then I risk losing my job.

Once mothers have overcome the obstacles to securing
day care and have begun working, they usually encounter
another series of problems, all of which are based on the
failure of employers and day care providers to accommodate the special needs of working mothers.

The working mother usually finds herself in a delicate ✓
and complex relationship with her employer. The most
basic characteristics an employer seeks in his employees are
dependability and resultant maximum productivity. Although capable of managing her own time schedule and
good health, the working mother nonetheless finds herself
at the mercy of her children's often time-consuming health
needs. Depending on the child care situation she has arranged for her children and on the understanding and
flexibility of her employer, the working mother finds herself caught in a conflict ranging from the inconvenient to
the traumatic. Having overcome the still current and usually subtle discrimination against women in hiring practices, salaries and working conditions, the working mother
faces additional threats to her job security. More than half
the mothers surveyed reported time lost from work because
of problems related to child care.

Employers differ greatly in their willingness to allow

mothers time off without undue penalty to care for the needs of their children. More than a third of the mothers' survey reported they could not take time off to take care of a sick child without fear of some subtle reprisal.

Despite contrary advice by the American Academy of Pediatrics, almost all child care centers, either by policy or through a lack of facilities, refuse to allow children with minor symptoms of illness to attend. Many mothers reported that they were called at work if their child vomited, had a mild fever or was slightly injured. Occurrences dealt with at home by no more than a comforting kiss, a reassuring pat or a brief period of rest are cause for the child care center staff to summon the child's parent from her job. Most mothers stay home from work when their child is ill, while others obtain a paid sitter. In either case, the child's illness becomes a substantial financial burden and occasionally even a threat to the mother's job:

> I take home $81.00 a week from my job. I pay $7.80 a week for the day care center. My son was sick for two days once, and I had to pay a sitter $32.00 to look after him. I couldn't take off from work because we had too many rush orders to fill. Something always comes up to keep me from getting ahead of the game.

Problems such as these prey on mothers' energies, creating dissatisfactions having nothing to do with the benefits they feel their children are receiving in day care programs. Most mothers readily acknowledge that the opportunities for their children to socialize with playmates, to relate to adults other than their parents and to share in even the most rudimentary educational experiences contribute substantially to their children's overall growth. Mothers seek evidence that the day care experience includes at least some of the indefinable qualities that traditionally have been a part only of home life. Foreign-born or ethnic-minority parents want their children exposed to their native language, customs and foods, to minimize the conflicts between home life and day care.

Since most of the mothers interviewed lived on the edge of welfare, most of them had dealings at one time or another with social agencies. They suffered the inevitable problems of red tape, occasional humiliation and general depersonalization. Almost above all else, they want their children spared these institutionalized and dehumanized situations. Mothers react strongly and resentfully to any encounter with day care providers that smacks of bureaucracy or indifference. Often nothing more than the crowded schedules of day care workers and the crush of parents competing for their attention at the end of the day lends this impression. Day care providers should be mindful of the sensitivities of the parents they serve.

Mothers seek indications that the nutritional, health, emotional and intellectual needs of their children receive the attention and concern of the day care workers. Their personal schedules and responsibilities rarely afford them the time to participate in the centers' activities, yet they eagerly seek word on their children's development and progress. Written communications between parents and the centers must improve until personal meetings can be arranged.

An important lesson of the survey was that mothers enthusiastically participated in the opportunity to have someone listen to their stories. Many of the mothers lived in near total isolation and sincerely doubted whether anyone cared what they had to say. The ignorance or insensitivity that day care providers, employers and the government often display toward the personal situations of the mothers and their children contribute to these doubts. Many mothers hesitated to criticize something they needed so desperately, yet most had very definite opinions that could be elicited only in friendly, informal talks with sincerely interested and sympathetic people.

From the results of the survey of mothers, we can safely

conclude that day care services will not meet the needs and expectations of parents until everyone involved in day care, including parents, providers, administrators and legislators make the extra effort to arrange face-to-face meetings and interviews with the people who most need the services of day care centers and homes.

THE SURVEY REPORT

The survey report brought to light many important facts concerning the identity, the needs and expectations of working mothers in San Francisco. The effort made to include mothers of different backgrounds from different neighborhoods involved with the full range of child care programs from OEO centers, to private centers, to day care homes ensured that the conclusions drawn from this can be applied to many communities.

Nearly two-thirds of the more than 125 mothers surveyed were between the ages of twenty and thirty, and seven out of eight of all the mothers had either one or two children under the age of five. Three out of five had no children over five years old.

Four-fifths of the women worked full time in a broad variety of occupations. Their children, therefore, needed all-day, full-week programs. Nearly half the mothers received free child care once they gained admission to a program, but the largest group of mothers (21 percent) other than those who received free child care paid over $25.00 per week.

Three-fifths of the mothers preferred their children to attend a child care center outside of, but near their home. Generally convenience was the most important consideration in selecting a child care center, especially since many mothers admitted that they did not know what to look for in a center or were too intimidated by the process to make a judgment based on program content. In any event, a substantial number made their final selection because they had no alternative.

Parents stressed outdoor play and preparation for school as the two most important aspects of their children's day care program. Activities fostering the child's social development and independence also received high priorities.

When asked what, in general terms, they expected from child care and whether they felt they were getting it, mothers focused on day care programs providing the same things a child would receive in his own home. Above all, the children should be safe from harm. Mothers do not want their children left unattended and expect a high degree of individual attention paid to them. Perhaps the greatest disadvantage mothers see in the whole idea of day care is the lack of a single adult on whom the children can depend completely. However, most mothers feel this is outweighed by many advantages. As one mother put it:

> For a long time I struggled with the idea that my first responsibility was to my child. That he needed me and my attention more than anything else, and that no one could take my place. Then I realized I was holding us both back. I figured maybe dealing with other adults and kids would be good for him. And it has been.

Similarly, another mother stated:

> As much as I felt Tina needed me, I realized I couldn't play with her as someone her own age could. I live pretty much alone, so if she didn't go to the center, she wouldn't have anyone to play with. Besides, I don't want her to get too dependent on me, because I need a little room to breathe, too.

Mothers expected that the children should be well nourished. The type and quantity of food disappointed many parents. Many of the mothers were on very limited budgets, and counted on the day care center to provide the greatest portion of their children's nutrition. Related to this, many parents felt that the children should eat a greater variety of foods, stressing foods native to their culture.

Mothers expected the day care centers to have a comprehensive health program, including screening, daily check-ups by staff, periodic visits by various health professionals and provisions for dealing with an ill child for at least a day. Many mothers counted on the day care center as the primary source of health attention for their children. One mother summed up the problem:

> I don't see my kid too much during the day, just in the morning when he's still sleepy, and at night, when he's tired from a long day. I can't tell too good whether his health is O.K. The ones who can are at the center, because they see him all day and can compare him to the other kids.

The diversity of ethnic groups—Latino, Filipino, Black and Chinese—raised a group of common demands among many mothers. One in six of all the mothers preferred that their children attend a child care center affiliated with either their racial, ethnic or religious group, and receive care according to their family traditions. Several of these mothers felt that their children would soon enough receive an American education and indoctrination, but that as young children they should receive a traditional upbringing. Although Latin, Chinese and Filipino mothers represented only a third of the sample, they almost unanimously mentioned the lack of a bilingual/ bicultural program and a bilingual staff. They felt their language and heritage were inadequately reinforced by the centers. In addition, they found that communicating with the staff was often difficult and doubted that the staff was able to understand their children's special needs. As one Chinese mother stated, through an interpreter:

> My kids don't know what to believe. They don't eat the same foods as at home. The teacher tells them not to hold their bowl up when they eat, and that's the only

way to eat with chopsticks. They don't sing the same songs and hear the same stories as at home. They don't celebrate our holidays.

Nine out of ten mothers felt that cultural experiences such as folk dancing, singing, different foods and stories in native (and in the case of Blacks and Whites, foreign) languages, and native food should be included in the program. Implied here was that parents wanted life at the child care center or home to resemble as closely as possible life in the children's own homes.

When asked to describe the most nearly ideal day care arrangement for their children, mothers preferred a moderate-sized day care center near their home. Their reasons for such a choice were similar:

> When my daughter is home with me, evenings and weekends, things are pretty quiet. During the day when I'm at work, I would like her to play with lots of other kids and get a chance to learn about as many different types of kids her own age as possible.

> I feel a medium-sized day care center offers the greatest variety of children and adults without being too large and impersonal, or too small and close.

The second choice was a small day care home in the family's neighborhood. Again mothers had similar reasons for this choice:

> I feel a young child needs as close to a home environment as possible, and a small day care home with no more than six children comes closest to the child's own home situation.

> I still think a kid needs a mother nearby, or someone who can act like a mother. A woman in her own home with a few kids can be a mother to all of them. Even though I've heard some stories about people who didn't know what they were doing running day care homes, I still think they're better for the kids.

> With a day care home you can get to know the
> operator better and feel closer to her. You can also get
> to know the other parents better, too. It's more like a
> big family.

Other mothers mentioned a problem that often is
overlooked, the lack of after-school programs and facilities
for schoolaged children. Hundreds of children in San
Francisco and other cities return to empty homes and
apartments to fend for themselves while their working
mothers worry about their safety.

The survey also revealed the reason for one of the day
care movement's greatest problems—the lack of a pool of
mothers with a long-term commitment to its cause. Most
mothers surveyed had only one or two children. Since
their direct involvement in day care programs and problems lasts, on the average, for only the two years that their
child is in a day care program before entering elementary
school, there is a tendency not to engage wholeheartedly
in the cause. Moreover, the frustrations are so great, and
the disappointments so frequent, that many mothers retreat in exhaustion after their two-year period of utilization is up. Mothers, who labor under an apparent lack of
progress during the period of their personal involvement,
and who are also continually having to deal with the full
range of time-consuming and energy-sapping problems
involved in managing a home and employment, tend to
drift away from the movement. The typical day care consumer rarely has the time or resources to develop a broad
understanding of the situation, and consequently the
movement and they have suffered from the lack of opportunity to contribute.

Unlike elementary school teachers, who have a well-
defined curriculum to present to a group of children of
the same age, the child care worker's responsibilities are
largely open ended. The child care worker is responsible
not so much for an educational program as for a social
service to the families in the program. In order to ac-

complish these goals, the child care worker must, through informal interviews such as those which resulted in this report, actively seek out the opinions and needs of the people in the community. Since the typical child care consumer leads a hectic and pressured existence, with little time and energy to initiate communications and activities with the day care center, child care workers must take the initiative to provide all parents with the information and reassurances they need. Only then will day care succeed in earning the enthusiastic support of parents and the public.

REFERENCES

American Academy of Pediatrics. *Recommendations for day care centers for infants and children.* Evanston, Ill.: American Academy of Pediatrics, 1973.

Auerbach-Fink, S. *Parents and child care: a report on child care consumers in San Francisco: a study of parental expectations for child care services from a cross cultural perspective.* San Francisco: Far West Laboratory, 1974.

Auerbach, S., Child care: a cruel hoax. *The Humanist,* Nov.-Dec., 1972.

Bronfenbrenner, U., *Day care U.S.A.: a statement of principles.* Washington, D.C.: Office of Child Development, 1972. Also available from the Day Care and Child Development Council of America.

Chandler, D. A., Lourie, R., & Peters, A. In L. L. Dittmann (Ed.), *Early child care: the new perspectives.* N.Y.: Atherton Press, 1968.

Frost, J. L. *Revisiting early childhood programs: readings.* N.Y.: Holt, Rinehart and Winston, 1973.

Hess, R. Parent involvement in early education in day care. In E. H. Grotberg (Ed.), *Resources for decisions.* Washington, D.C.: Office of Economic Opportunity, 1972. Also available from the Day Care and Child Development Council of America.

Roby, P. (Ed.) *Child Care: Who cares? Foreign and domestic infant and early childhood development policies.* N.Y.: Basic Books, 1973.

Ruderman, F. A. *Child care and working mothers.* N.Y.: Child Welfare League of America, 1968.

Yudkin, S. & Holme, A. *Working mothers and their children.* London: Michael Joseph, Ltd., 1963.

APPENDIX

DEVELOPMENTAL CHILD CARE SERVICES

Report of Forum 17
1970 White House Conference on Children

PARTICIPANTS

Dr. Jerome Kagan (Mass.)   Mr. Kino Gonzalez (Colo.)
Mr. Richard Lansburgh (Md.) Rev. Oddie Hoover (Ohio)
Mr. Paul Boswell (Ill.)   Ms. Ruth Jefferson (Fla.)
Dr. Bettye Caldwell (Ala.)   Mr. Earnest Lugo (Cal.)
Luis Diaz De Leon (Tex.)   Ms. Mary Robinson (Md.)
Dr. Donald Fink (Cal.)   Ms. Evelyn Moore (Mich.)
Mr. W. E. Finlayson (Wisc.)   Jule Sugarman (N.Y.)
Ms. Almavine Garcia (P.R.)   Mr. William Barton (Tenn.)

Staff Associate: Charles Super (Mass.)
Govt. Representative: Stevanne Auerbach (Wash. D.C.)

INTRODUCTION

The members and delegates of this forum (representing
private, state, local, and parent organizations,
business, and private industry throughout the nation)
are shocked at the lack of national attention to the
critical developmental needs of children. We urge
the recognition of day care as a developmental service
with tremendous potential for positively influencing
and strengthening the lives of children and families,
and we urge the eradication of day care as only a
custodial, "baby-sitting" service.

The fundamental issue is how we can arrange for the
optimal nurturance of today's children at a time of
profound change in the American family and its living
conditions. The responses to the changing needs of
children, families, and communities have been a
variety of part-time child care arrangements outside
the family. Too many of these ideas and experiments
are isolated from each other and from existing
community resources. Too often, thought about such
programs is fragmented into restricted concepts --
nursery schools, babysitting, preschool enrichment
centers, or child care service for parents in job
training. These programs are not a full solution,
but are individual responses to parts of a general
and growing national need for supplementary child
care services.

Although this paper considers the broad range of
needs, it focuses on developmental child care which
we define as any care, supervision, and developmental
opportunity for children which supplements parental
care and guidance. The responsibility for such
supplementary care is delegated by parents (or guardians) and generally provided in their absence; however,
the home and family remain the central focus of the
child's life. Parents must retain the primary responsibility for rearing their children; but society, in
turn, must recognize its role in the ultimate responsibility for the child's well-being and development.

Developmental child care should meet not only normal
supervisory, physical, health, and safety needs, but
should also provide for the intellectual, social,
emotional, and physical growth and development of the
child with opportunities for parental involvement and
participation. Day care can be provided in public
and private day care centers, Head Start programs,
nursery schools, day nurseries, kindergartens, and

family day care homes, as well as before and after
school, and during vacations.

Child care is a service for all children -- infants,
toddlers, preschoolers, and school-age children.
Regardless of the hours, the auspices, the funding
source, the name of the service, or the child's
age, the program should be judged by its success in
helping each child develop tools for learning and
growing, both in relation to his own life style and
abilities and in the context of the larger culture
surrounding him.

THE NEED: SOME DATA

Many forces are converging to accelerate the need for
day care: female employment; family mobility; urban-
ization; community mobilization to fight poverty;
the rise in single-parent families through divorce,
separation, or other causes; pressures to reduce the
public welfare burden; and realization of the needs
and opportunities for early education in the broadest
sense.

The most direct force is the growing number of
employed women. Since the beginning of World War II,
mothers have increased almost eightfold.(1)   Today
half of the nation's mothers with school-age children
are working at least part-time (a third with children
under six years),(2) and by the 1980 White House
Conference on Children, working mothers of preschool
children alone are expected to increase by over one
and one-half million.(3)   Although the primary motive
for women to work is economic -- to provide or help
provide food, housing, medical care, and education
for their families (4) -- increasing numbers of women
work for the personal satisfaction of using their education, skills, and creativity. Many more women, often
those with critically needed skills, such as nurses,
would work if they could be sure of adequate care for
their children.(5)   More women are demanding more
choices in their lives: choices in parenthood, in
jobs, and in family roles. The result -- more than
twelve million children under fourteen had mothers
working at least part-time in 1965; four and one-half
million of these children were under six.

What happened to those children while their mothers
worked? Thirteen percent required no supplementary

care since their mothers worked only while they were
in school. For the remaining eighty-seven percent,
a variety of arrangements were used. Forty-six percent
were cared for at home by the father, another adult
relative, a sibling (often a child himself), or
someone paid to come into the home. Fifteen percent
were cared for by their mothers on the job, and sixteen
percent were cared for away from home, half by a
relative and half in small "family day care homes."
Only two percent of the children received group care
in a day care center or nursery school, and eight
percent received no care at all (including 18,000
preschoolers).(6)   These percentages vary, of course,
for the different age groups. The complete picture
of supplementary care must also include the hundreds
of thousands of children attending nursery school
whose mothers do not work.(7)

If all these care arrangements were adequate, we
would have to worry only about the almost one million
"latch-key" children who received no care. But many
of these care arrangements do not even assure immediate
physical safety, as child accident rates show. We
know very little of the quality of care given by
non-maternal sources in the home, but of the outside
arrangements, far too many are unlicensed, unsuper-
vised, and chosen because they are the only available
care alternative. Even the many dedicated women who
put effort and love into their "family care" or
nursery school often lack the training and the educational, medical, physical, and financial resources
to meet the needs of a growing child. A recent nationwide survey of child care has turned up far too many
horrifying examples of children neglected and endan-
gered in both licensed and unlicensed centers.(8)
In a study of New York City, eighty percent of the
known and inspected day care homes were rated as
inadequate.(9)   Since the major failings were related
to inadequate resources and physical facilities and
since the homes were in the child's neighborhood,
it is reasonable to assume that other neighborhood
home care sites, including the child's own home,
would rate no better using the same criteria.

The dramatic rise in the need for child care services
caused by changing employment patterns has partly
overshadowed the great needs evident since well before
the first White House Conference on Children in 1910.
Special programs are required to serve the needs of
children suffering emotional disturbance, mental
retardation, cerebral palsy, and other handicaps; to
assist families with such children by relieving the

parents of some of the burdens of full-time care;
and to help strengthen families in difficult situations
by offering child care and attention perhaps otherwise
unobtainable. These needs still exist, and in large
numbers. Over eleven percent of school-age children
have emotional problems requiring some type of mental
health service.(10) The vast majority of these five
million children, and preschoolers with similar problems, can be treated by trained professionals and
paraprofessionals "working in settings not primarily
established for treatment of mental illness."(11)
Three million persons under the age of 20 are mentally
retarded; with adequate training and continued support,
most could learn to care for themselves, but special
education classes reach only a quarter of those needing
them.(12) Similarly, many of the thousands of families
with children handicapped by blindness, cerebral palsy,
and other disorders, are unable to find the necessary
assistance in caring for their children. Partly in
response to these facts, the recent Joint Commission
on Mental Health of Children recommended the "creation
or enlargement of day care and preschool programs"
as a major preventive service, with an important
potential role in crisis intervention and treatment
services.(13) These programs, they said, should be
"available as a *public utility* to all children."(14)

For all these needs, about 640,000 spaces for children
presently exist in licensed day care homes and centers.
But this number compares to a need estimated at several
million.(15) Even though the number of places has
risen rapidly in the past five years -- from 250,000
to 640,000 -- the total picture has improved little;
while the 400,000 places were being added, the number
of children under age six whose mothers were working
increased by 800,000.(16)

ANSWERS OLD AND NEW

The social institutions traditionally responsible for
child care have generally treated the new needs simply
as more of the old. For decades, "day care" has been
part of "child welfare," where it has been "tended
by a devoted few, condescended to by many." It is
still widely believed that only mothers on the verge
of destitution seek employment and outside care for
their children; that only disintegrated families,
where parents are unfit to give even minimal care,
seek outside support. The need for supplementary

child care is often viewed as the result of other pathology in the family, its use justified only in forestalling greater disaster for the child.(17)

The child welfare concept of day care -- as a service to poor and problem families -- has contributed to the resistance to enlarging services to cover broader segments of the population. Inadequately funded and primarily concerned with the care and protection of children, agencies have usually responded by creating supervised centers for care, and/or promoting additional regulation and licensing of less formal child care arrangements.

Both approaches have failed to meet the current demand for day care arrangements. Although thousands of families are unable to find care for their children, some group care centers show serious under-enrollment. One study found that nearly three-quarters of the centers in one city had spaces available; the same study found only 250 officially approved and licensed day care homes serving the community, compared to several thousand women providing care in informal and unregulated arrangements.(18)

The reasons that the traditional responses have touched only a minor part of the present supplementary child care needs are complex, but include lack of community understanding of, and commitment to child care, inadequate community coordination and information on available programs, the high cost of center care, and parental preference for convenient and personal arrangements. This points to a need for sponsoring agencies to be flexible and responsive to family needs. Families must be encouraged to understand and seek quality care. The needs and uses of child care services have changed more rapidly than our understanding of the situation and our ability to respond to it.

The point is that developmental child care is no longer needed primarily to buttress disintegrating families. Economics, divorce, education, cultural values, and other factors have led to' a variety of family situations. The working mother is no longer a "misfit," and the family is not the simple mother-father-child picture usually assumed. By the end of this decade, it is possible that most American children will have working mothers, and there is no reason to think these mothers will be less concerned than other mothers about the care their children receive, or that their employment will, of itself, lead to destructive deviations from normal parent-child relationships.(19)

Because the primary need for child care is to help
functioning families lead more satisfying lives, and
not to replace families, services which are not
responsive to the variety of family needs will not
be adequate. We must understand the process by which
families choose a particular child care arrangement.
In general, they are looking for supplementary care
that is flexible in hours, reasonable in cost, convenient in location, and, often last, dependable in
quality.(20)   The challenge we face is to develop a
system of services with at least three effects: making
parents more aware of quality in child care programs;
assisting parents in maintaining their parental
responsibilities; and delivering good care to all
children, regardless of the specific arrangement.

Although as a nation we lack an adequate system of
developmental child care services, many local efforts
have been fruitful during the past decades. Thousands
of children and families have benefited from the
programs developed and sponsored by church groups,
parent cooperatives, community organizations, and
small proprietary operations. As more services are
developed, the progress and wisdom gained from
successful efforts must not be lost.

A New Force: Child Development

Next to the growing number of employed women, the
second force in the increasing demand for making
available supplementary child care to all citizens
grows out of recent discoveries on the importance of
early experience on human growth and development.
Psychologists, pediatricians, psychiatrists, educators,
nutritionists, anthropologists, and other investigators
continue to document the critical significance of
the first years of life. The central finding is
that during the years when a child's body, intellect,
and psyche are developing most rapidly, his conditions
of life will profundly influence his later health,
motivations, intelligence, self-image, and relations
to other people.(21)

Every moment of a child's life is learning -- what
he can and cannot do, what adults expect and think
of him, what people need and like and hate, what his
role in society will be. His best chances for a
satisfying and constructive adulthood grow from a
satisfying and constructive childhood and infancy.

Sound development cannot be promoted too early for
the early experiences will be either supportive or
destructive. The President's Commission on Mental
Retardation estimated that three-quarters of mental
retardation in America could not be related directly
to genetics (such as mongolism or Down's syndrome),
physical damage, or other organic factors and was
typically associated with geographic areas, where
health care, nutrition, and developmental opportunities
are usually minimal.(22)

One reason why many social institutions formerly
resisted extra-familial child care was their deep
belief in the importance of family life and fear of
the possibly destructive results of separating a
child from his mother. The institutional syndrome
of maternal deprivation found in many orphanages was
attributed to any separation from the biological
mother, rather than to prolonged separation combined
with other institutional conditions such as perceptual
monotony; little interaction with adults; and lack
of a basis for self, family, and historical identity.
Traditional guidelines viewed day care as a last
resort because the institutional findings were over-
generalized to include the part-time -- and very
different -- separation involved in day care, where
the child returns daily to the family.(23)

While it remains supremely important to ensure against
deprivation of adult care, it now appears that with
adequate planning even full day care can sustain
the emotional adjustment of infants and leave intact
their attachment to the mother.(24) In addition, it
is becoming clear that day care holds an important
potential for providing all children with "the essentials of experience" which support optimal development.
Although until recently few attempts were made to
evaluate objectively the efforts of full day care,
abundant research documents the possibility of desirable effects associated with some variety of experience
outside the home which involves careful planning of
the environment for the young child.(25) New research
is accumulating to demonstrate that day care projects
can provide programs highly beneficial to the social
and intellectual functioning of children.(26) When
programs are successfully integrated with, and followed
up by, the public school system, the possibility of
maintaining these advantages remains high.

It is also important to realize that the *place* where
care is given is not the most significant dimension
for a child. The issue is the *kind* of care given:

how he is handled, what abilities are nurtured, what
values are learned, and what attitudes toward people
are acquired. The child can learn to trust or hate
in a neighbor's apartment, in a commune, in an expensive nursery school, or in his own house. Parents
have realized this, and their fear of exposing their
children to destructive influences, along with a widespread misunderstanding of children's needs and their
relationship to our particular nuclear family arrangement, have tied "women more tightly to their children
than has been thought necessary since the invention
of bottle feeding and baby carriages."(27)

Our traditional model of the biological mother as the
sole and constant caretaker is, in fact, unusual.
In most cultures and in most centuries, care has been
divided among the mother, father, sisters, brothers,
aunts, grandparents, cousins, and neighbors. Universal
education for older children, the geographic mobility
of families, and the social isolation of many people
in the cities have drastically limited these resources
for the American mother. As a result, we are now
faced with the need for new options for child care.
The "day care" option involves placing the child for
a substantial part of his day in the care of a person
who initially has no close social relationship with
the family. Like the location of care, this may be
of little importance by itself -- it is the developmental concern of the care, whatever its source,
which is the world of the child and which influences
the future adult.

Day care is a powerful institution. Quality service
geared to the needs and abilities of each child can
be an enormously constructive influence. But a poorly
funded program, where children are left with few
challenging activities and have little relationship
with or guidance from adults, can seriously jeop-
ardize development. A day care program that ministers
to a child from six months to six years of age has
over 8,000 hours to teach him values, fears, beliefs,
and behaviors. Therefore, the question of what kinds
of people we want our children to become must guide
our view of day care. Scientific knowledge can point
to several possible dangers and can suggest principles
for sound programs. But the program which best suits
a particular child in a given community cannot be
predicted in any precise way. After all formal
standards and guidelines have been met, parents and
organizations must still remain open and responsive
to the needs of individual children.

Child care programs cannot hope to meet the needs of children unless they are responsive to parents' values and their understanding of their own children. Similarly, parents can learn a great deal about meeting the needs of their children by remaining open to new knowledge about child development. One of the socially beneficial aspects of a day care program is that it provides a forum for parents and staff to pursue jointly new understandings to guide child-rearing endeavors.

Day Care, Politics, and Reality

A third factor behind the concern with day care is pragmatic. A growing number of mothers want to work and will seek the benefits of good care for their children and for themselves. In addition, such programs as Head Start have made the public aware of the vast potentials which can be realized if we commit ourselves and our country to providing a sufficient number of quality programs which encourage a new vigor for life in children, families, and communities.

Given a taste of such programs, the public is becoming anxious for continuation and expansion. To discuss at length whether day care is an economic luxury, a political right, or a social tool ignores the tremendous need for supplementary care which exists today, a need which parents will continue to meet the best they can with whatever resources are available. *The question is not whether America "should" have day care, but rather whether the day care which we do have, and will have, will be good -- good for the child, good for the family, and good for the nation.*

As with any question of economic and social resources, people with the least private access to them deserve primary consideration in the allocation of public resources. Good developmental child care can cost $2,000 to $5,000 per year, and even most middle-class families cannot bear such costs.(28) Sliding scales for payment -- from 0 to 100 percent -- must be developed to enable all citizens to participate as we build toward a system of developmental child care available to all parents who seek it and all children who need it.

The ability to pay for care, though, is not the same issue as the need to find care. There are many

segments of society which need supplementary developmental child care. Employment rates are higher for
mothers who are the sole support of their children,
and higher for those whose husbands earn less than
$3,000 a year; but most working mothers have working
husbands earning more than $5,000 a year. The most
rapid rise in seeking work and child care is occurring
in the group of mothers with the most education.(29)
The problem facing our public and private institutions
is to organize and pay for good services for all
families.

THE CHALLENGE

There are two clear issues in developmental child
care for American children: the comprehensiveness and
quality of care which all children deserve; and the
responsiveness and flexibility of social institutions
to the changing needs and desires of American parents.
The best care, with stimulating and nurturing personnel,
will be wasted if offered in programs which will not
be used by families as they adjust their own social,
economic, and personal needs. Simply keeping the
child during parents' working hours without applying
our utmost expertise and common sense for his sound
development is as cruel and absurd as feeding him
only minimal nutrition required to sustain life and
expecting a vigorous and healthy body. We need not
just day care centers so mothers can work, nor just
preschools. Rather, we must respond as a nation to
the changes that we as individuals are living, changes
in our views of family roles and in the needs of our
families with children. Our lives are changing more
rapidly than our institutions. We must develop a
network of voluntary supplementary child care, flexible enough to be part of family life, able to promote
the full development of our children, and readily
available to all families with children. We must
commit our heads, our hearts, and our pocketbooks to
this task.

PLANNING SUPPLEMENTARY CHILD CARE SERVICES

Forum 17 believes that the following points should
be carefully considered in planning developmental
child care services.

Settings and Facilities

Although the location of child care is not a crucial factor, different settings can influence how well a particular service fits the needs of a family. For example, a center for children of two to six years adjacent to a factory may be useful in some circumstances. But problems will arise if the mother of a three-year-old also has an infant or a school-age child, who will need some other care; or if the mother changes jobs, and the child is no longer eligible for that center; or if difficult public transportation must be used. For a mother who works short hours, the family day care home run by a neighbor or a home-visiting service operating out of a child care center may be most useful. Families which must move frequently -- migrant and seasonal workers, military personnel, and so on -- face additional problems. Special settings may also be needed for evening care for children whose parents work unusual hours; or for short-term, crisis care in the case of death, illness, or arrest of a parent.

It is important that facilities "feel comfortable" to the children they serve. Ramps and other aspects of design may appreciably improve the handicapped child's view of his importance and belonging in the center. For normal children, too, one goal of design should be to foster their development; there is much room for innovation here. Facilities also have a role in the community; store-front, split-level modern, or whatever, a child care center should fit its community's view of what is appropriate and important.

The lack of funds for renovating and constructing facilities has inhibited the growth of more and innovative services. If a program must be revised to accommodate limitations of the available settings, crucial program elements for the child or the family may be slighted or eliminated. Every effort, therefore, must be made to provide facilities and settings for the services which encourage program flexibility and quality and are most appropriate to a given set of needs.

Personnel

There are not enough trained day care personnel to staff current programs, and expanding the services

will increase this shortage. If half the four- and
five-year-old children of working mothers were served
by programs following the Federal Inter-agency Standards ratio of one adult to five children, over
35,000 trained personnel would be needed to staff
those programs alone.

Recent attempts to define the skills needed by these
workers have stressed general human abilities and
sympathies, and specific training in child development,
family relations, and community involvement. The need
for persons with a variety of expertise suggests that
active cooperation between educational institutions,
local businesses, and individuals in the community
can be very profitable. Academic training is by no
means necessary for all persons who work with young
children, but experience and training are essential
for directors and head teachers if children are to
receive quality care. In-service training of local
persons has proven a valuable procedure for many day
care programs, serving the joint purpose of producing
excellent staff who know the life situation of the
children and of using resources efficiently. Local
colleges often help with planning and running the
training programs and provide academic credit for
those interested and able to develop careers in the
field. Such career ladders are an important part of
training programs. New roles are also needed for
workers, both in terms of the duties they perform
and the persons who fill them. Some programs are
now being developed for personnel to administer
basic health services and other program elements.
Teenagers and older citizens, both male and female,
can also work in programs to the benefit of both
themselves and the children.

PROGRAMS

In the end, the content of a child care program is
most important to the development of the child.
Children need to learn social and intellectual
attitudes and skills that will enable them to cope
successfully with society and meet their own individual
needs. A good program, then, must attend to all
areas of growth: social, physical, emotional, intellectual, and spiritual. How these elements are
combined in the program will depend heavily on such
factors as the type of service and the other developmental resources of the community. Several points
stand out, however, as especially important.

--A good program must focus on the development of
warm, trusting, and mutually respectful social
relationships with adults and other children.
Such relationships form the basis not only for
the social and personal development of the child,
but also for his future ability to learn from
others.

--The program must help develop self-identity so
that each child views himself and his background
as worthy of respect and dignity. A child's
image of himself as a member of a racial,
cultural, linguistic, religious, or economic
group is basic to a strong self-concept.
Cultural relevance, therefore, is not a separate
political issue but an integral part of human
development. Supplementary child care must
not alienate a child from his family and his
peers. Those in charge of programs must be
knowledgeable of and sensitive to the values
and patterns of life in the children's homes.
To help correct past inadequacies and injustices
and move toward a truly human heritage for
future generations, children must also learn
about our diverse cultures and their contributions
to modern America.

--Provisions must be made to ensure nutrition and
health care that focus on promotion of optimal
health and prevention of disease, as well as
the identification, evaluation, and treatment
of existing health problems. Integration of
health services with other child care services
is essential.

--Attention must be given to the full development
of each child, taking into account his or her
individual ability, personality, imagination,
and independence, and resisting the degradation
caused by racist, sexist, economic, cultural,
and other stereotypes.

--A good program should utilize the knowledge and
resources of those trained in, and familiar
with, child development to foster the maximum
potential of each child as well as to utilize
their knowledge for selection and use of equipment, space, and methods to achieve the desired
goals in a comprehensive child care program.

--The inclusion of parents in the affairs of the
program is a vital element in the value of the

program.(31)   It is important that families
maintain the feeling of responsibility for,
and involvement with, their children. Parental
participation can be at several levels, depending on the particular family's skills and available time. The aim is mutually beneficial communication between the program and the parents.
Parental control of fundamental aspects of the
program is also important; this is one reason
informal and private arrangements are preferred
by many parents.

--In institutionalized group care facilities,
especially when supported by public funds, legal
issues may become complicated, but they nevertheless remain secondary to the principle that
child care centers, like governments, are
instituted to serve the people. The power of
control, therefore, should ultimately rest with
those affected by the programs. Children, whose
lives are the most affected, cannot vote for
either policy-making bodies or public officials,
but they must not be forgotten. One concern of
day care as an institution should be to act as
a voice for children.

LICENSING

The licensing of out-of-home care for children can
serve the dual purposes of protecting children and
their families from inadequate care and of helping
agencies and individuals improve their programs
through providing, promoting, or coordinating training for staff in administration, program planning,
and daily interaction and understanding of children.
Unfortunately, many licensing authorities do not
live up to these possibilities because regulations
are inappropriate or because their own training and
funding are inadequate. In some cases, the complexity
of local, state, and other requirements impedes the
establishment and expansion of programs, both good
and bad. Too often, regulations focus on physical
facilities and on superficial differences in services,
such as "nursery schools" versus "day care centers,"
and ignore crucial areas such as the inclusion of
specific program elements. The creation of licensing
agencies with the resources and power to take strong
action against harmful programs and equally strong
action for better care is one of the most important
challenges in working for a flexible network of
quality child care services.

Organization for the Delivery of Service

The need for coordination in the delivery of services arises in every discussion of day care needs.
We see the goals as coordination and consolidation
at upper levels, with coordination, diversity, and
flexibility at local levels.

Although the Federal government is making efforts
at coordinated planning through such actions as the
Community Coordinated Child Care Program (4C), designed by the Federal Panel on Early Childhood, it
is currently operating over 60 different funding
programs for child care or child development.
Among these, there are at least seven separate programs with funds for operating expenses, nine personnel training programs, seven research programs,
four food programs, and three loan programs. Only
a few of these, however, are aimed directly at child
development; most were set up for other purposes
and day care or child development is only ancillary.
Funding, moreover, is grossly inadequate, and state
and local support is, with rare exceptions, minimal
or non-existent.

As a result of such overlap, child care centers
funded by different sources could compete for the
same children. In other cases, proposed and
needed centers cannot get funded. Lack of coordination may mean frequent placement changes for children. And, ironically, the complexity of sources
can result in sorely needed funds remaining un-
known and unused.

One solution to this set of problems would be to
establish a Federal mechanism for consolidation,
and local structures for coordination and diversity.

At the Federal level, consolidation of administrative responsibility for children's programs is
urgently needed. The present administration has
taken a significant step in establishing the Office
of Child Development (OCD) and assigning to it responsibility for day care services. However, the
responsibilities have not yet been designated for
all programs concerned with early childhood development. Thus, Head Start and other programs could
remain within OCD, while day care services delivered as part of the Family Assistance Plan could
operate quite separately. This arrangement would
violate both the ethical and scientific arguments
against segregating children on the basis of financial need. Furthermore, health, educational, psy-

chological, and social services are all part of
the many-faceted approach which early childhood
programs should include. Developmental day care
services should be consolidated in one arm of the
Federal government, charged with general responsibility for all aspects of child development. Child
development programs should focus on the child, not
on his parents' status or on a bureaucratic division.

At the state and local level, maximum flexibility
is needed and is compatible with a democratic form
of government. To provide for diversity of programming and sponsorships which can best meet the
needs of each community, parent, and child, a
mechanism should be established to coordinate the
several branches of government involved in the
provision of day care services; non-public agencies,
involved either directly or indirectly; and a substantial number of parents. Such a coordinative
arrangement would serve to share knowledge of funding sources, to process information on the establishment and operation of programs, and to central-
ize such resources as training and purchasing. A
community-wide planning process would determine
the priorities of need and funding which would ensure both the continuity of services and the
generation of new programs.

The need for supplementary child care services is
so great that only by cooperation of all parties
can it be met. Estimates of the cost for the immediate unmet needs are on the order of two to four
billion dollars a year. Only the Federal government can mobilize such funds on a coordinated
basis; but other sources, public and private, will
also be vitally needed for the foreseeable future.
Industry, business, and the university can be especially helpful by contributing expertise in organization, accounting, training, and other areas
to local and state planning groups. They may also
play a special role by supplying starting funds and
some operating expenses to community child care
services in return for a guaranteed number of
places for the children of their employees.

Recommendations

ACTION FOR DEVELOPMENT CHILD CARE SERVICES

We recommend that a diverse national network of

*comprehensive developmental child care services be
established to accommodate approximately 5.6
million children by 1980 through consolidated
Federal efforts via legislation and funding, as
well as through coordinated planning and operation
involving state, local, and private efforts.*

The network's ultimate goal is to make high quality
care available to all families who seek it and all
children who need it.   By 1980 it should be prepared to accommodate approximately 5.6 million of
the estimated 57 million children potentially requiring developmental day care services, at a
yearly cost of approximately $10 billion.   Immedi-
ate efforts should be made to accommodate at least
500,000 children in each age group (infants, preschool, and school-age).   These efforts will require
$2 to $2.5 billion of Federal money per year, assuming that this amount can be matched from nonfederal sources, local, state, and private.

Such a network must be comprehensive in services,
including at least educational, psychological,
health, nutritional, and social services; and the
services must support family life by ensuring parent participation and involvement as well as including a cooperative parent education program.

The network must offer a variety of services including, where appropriate, group day care, family
care, and home care as well as evening and emergency care.   Services must cover all age groups
from infants through elementary school age.

Local coordination of child care services through
a Neighborhood Family and Child Center should be
strongly considered whenever appropriate. The
Center would:

   --Offer all the comprehensive and supplementary
     services outlined above.

   --Serve as an outlet for other programs and
     services and as a meeting place for parent
     and youth groups so that it may help create
     a community without alienation and separation.

Enabling comprehensive Federal legislation must not
only provide funds adequate for operating programs
(up to 100 percent where necessary) at the levels
projected above, but legislation must also:

   --Establish child care services independently

of public welfare, ensuring integration of
services to all ethnic and socioeconomic
groups

--Include funds for planning, support services,
training and technical assistance; facility
construction and renovation; coordination of
programs at Federal, state, and local levels;
research and development; and evaluation and
monitoring

--Ensure program continuity through long-term
grants and contracts.

The need for private capital in efforts to develop
the system is recognized. This forum approves
this involvement only if quality is maintained in
all areas affecting the child and/or his family.
The use of private funds should be encouraged by:
legislation to provide low-cost loans for facility
construction and renovation; tax incentives to the
private sector to develop quality child care services; and alteration of tax schedules to provide
tax relief to families who have children in developmental care.

While working toward the above goal, first priority
for spaces should go to children and families in
greatest need, whether the need be economic,
physical, emotional, or social. One hundred percent
funding should be made available for those who cannot afford quality child care; a sliding scale
should also be available to those above the poverty
level who are unable to bear full cost of the same
developmental opportunities as those given children
who must be fully subsidized by public funding.

Coordination of services should be ensured through
consolidation of all Federal activities relating to
child development in the Office of Child Development, and by coordination and planning by state and
local bodies. When a state's efforts are unable to
meet the needs of its children, direct Federal
funding to local projects should be required.

To hasten the achievement of this network, all construction of housing, business, industry, and service facilities (such as hospitals) which receive
Federal funds should be required to provide developmental child care services, either by including
such services in the construction or ensuring permanent funds for participation in existing or
planned facilities.

All child care centers and services should abide by
local, state, and Federal laws that apply to non-
discrimination in programming, housing, and construction of new buildings. Day care centers should
make every effort to support businesses that have
non-discriminatory practices.

ENSURE QUALITY OF CHILD CARE SERVICES

*We recommend that the quality of child care ser-
vices in America be ensured through innovative and
comprehensive training of child care personnel in
adequate numbers; parent and community control of
services; and supportive monitoring of services
and programs with enforcement of appropriate
standards.*

To ensure adequate personnel:

--The Federal government should fund and
   coordinate a combined effort by all levels of
   government, educational institutions, the
   private sector, and existing child care organizations to train at least 50,000 additional child care workers annually over the
   next decade.

--Education should be provided for training
   staff, professionals, preprofessionals, and
   volunteer staff who work directly with children; administrative and ancillary staff of
   child care programs; and parents.

--Special training for parenthood should be instituted in all public school systems, starting before junior high school. It should provide direct experience in child care centers
   and should include both male and female
   students.

--Joint efforts by educational institutions and
   existing child care services should be directed
   at creating new types of child care workers
   for child care settings. These new positions
   could be in areas such as health, child development, education, evaluation, and community
   services.

--Educational institutions should ensure
   transferability of training credits in child
   care; issue certificates of training which are

nationally recognized; and establish a consistent system of academic credit for direct
work experience.

--Child care institutions should allow paid
periods for continuing training and career
development. Funding for this policy should
be required in all Federal grants for child
care service operations.

To ensure that the system is responsive to demands
for quality care:

--Parents of enrolled children must control the
program at least by having the power to hire
and fire the director and by being consulted
on other positions.

--Parent and local communities must also control
local distribution of funds and community
planning and coordination.

To ensure the continuing quality of child care:

--Standards for service facilities and program
elements must apply to all child care services,
regardless of funding or auspices.

--Standards must be appropriate to the cultural
and geographic areas, the types of care, and
the available resources.

--Parents and other community members must play
a role in the flexible administration of
standards, licensing, and monitoring.

--Licensing should allow for some provisional
status while the service is being built up,
to enable programs to receive full funding.

--Federal and/or state governments should provide funds for training monitoring personnel.
These personnel must be numerous enough both
to observe the services in their area and to
work for their improvement.

NATIONAL PUBLIC EDUCATION CAMPAIGN

*We recommend a national campaign, coordinated and
funded by a Federal task force, to broaden public
understanding of child care needs and services.*

The campaign should be directed by a task force
of citizens representing the breadth of economic
and cultural groups in America who are concerned
with the issues of developmental child care services.

Using Federal monies, the task force should contract
with several private, non-profit organizations
(such as the Day Care and Child Development Council
of America, the Black Child Development Institute,
the Child Welfare League of America, and the
National Association for the Education of Young
Children) to prepare and disseminate to the general
public and specific institutions information concerning the difficulties, values, needs, costs,
and technicalities of child care services. Consumer education for informed selection of child
care services should be a major element of the
campaign. The campaign should use all forms of
media.

The task force should prepare and make public an
annual report evaluating its activities and contracts. A cumulative report should be presented
to the 1980 White House Conference on Children.

The task force should operate through the Office of
Child Development and should feed back to that office any information it receives concerning the
public's need for developmental child care services.

The Federal government should additionally contribute to public awareness by providing child care
facilities at all Federally sponsored conferences
and conventions, including the 1980 White House
Conference on Children.

The task force should encourage business and industry to make it easier to be both an employee and
a good parent. For example, job hours should be
flexible wherever possible, and more part-time jobs,
for both male and female, should be made available
with prestige and security equal to full-time jobs.

RESOLUTIONS BY FORUM 17 DELEGATES

We hereby change the title of Forum 17 from "Developmental Day Care Services for Children" to
"Developmental Child Care Services." (The title of
Forum 17 was changed by unanimous vote in order to
stress that the needs of children and families with

which we are concerned are not restricted to
daytime hours, and that child care must always be
developmental, not simply custodial. The content
of the paper should make it clear that we are not
discussing "child care services" in the sense of
adoption, foster homes, or institutional care.)

We, the Developmental Child Care Forum of the 1970
White House Conference on Children, find the
Federal Child Care Corporation Act, S. 4101,
inadequate and urge its defeat.

S. 4101 (Senator Long's Bill) does not address the
basic problem of providing operating funds. Nor
does it provide an acceptable delivery system
which must place the decision-making authority at
the local level and give parents a decisive role
in the policy direction of those programs in which
their children participate.

As a matter of principle, we do not believe that
program standards should ever be written into law.
S. 4101 would not only fix standards in law, but
would provide for such minimal standards that it
would allow the widespread public funding of
custodial programs which we vigorously oppose.

Society has the ultimate responsibility for the
well-being and optimum development of all children.
The implementation of this responsibility requires
that child development services such as day care,
Head Start, and after-school programs, be available
in all the variety of forms to meet the needs of
all children whose parents or guardians request,
or whose circumstances require, such services. In
further implementation of this concept, we propose
that all child development services be completely
separated from public assistance programs. They
must not be developed to lessen public assistance
roles but rather as a basic right.

We applaud the President's stated commitment to the
healthy development of young children. We believe
that the creation of the Office of Child Development has been an important first step in fulfilling
this commitment but further steps have not been
evident.

We strongly recommend that the administration now
act to provide the necessary resources to implement this commitment. The Office of Child Development must be enabled to meet its appropriate

responsibilities, including action on the recommendations of the White House conference.

We support the plan for a children's lobby presented by J. Sugarman, as amended.

We support the recommendations of the Spanish-
speaking, Spanish-surname caucus, especially those
most relevant to Forum 17 and as amended by it; to
wit:

To ensure that the specific concerns of the Spanish speaking children of the nation not be neglected and that the issues pertinent to groups such as Spanish-speaking American Indians and Black Americans not be diffused, the Spanish-speaking caucus makes the following recommendations.

Para asegurar que los intereses de los niños de habla-Hispana de la nación no sean depreciados y que los puntos importantes a este grupo no sean olvidos el caucus de personas de habla Española y de nombres Hispanos sugiere las siguientes recomendaciones.

Multilingual, multicultural education must be provided in the schools, on radio, and television, wherever five percent of the child population is of more than one culture.

El sistema educacional del pais, asi como las radio difusoras, televisión y todo medio de comunicación tiene que levar a cabo programas multilinguales multiculturales dondequiera que el 5% de la población de niños representa mas de una cultura.

Among the most disadvantaged children in the United States are the children of Spanish-speaking and Spanish-surname migrant workers. The highest priorities must be placed on immediate implementation of an extensive and comprehensive program to deal with the health, education, welfare, and labor problems faced by

Entre los niños de mayores necesidades básicas de los Estados Unidos se encuentran los niños de habla y tradición Hispana, que son hijos de trabajadores de labor en agricultura (migratorio y temporal). Debe prestarse altas prioridades a un programa extenso y comprehensivo de ayudar a resolver

these children and their
parents.

The child care and child
development programs must
be controlled at the com-
munity and neighborhood
level by the parents of
the children served so
as to ensure the child
an environment akin to
his cultural and ethnic
heritage. Services must
be divorced from welfare
agencies and must not be
used to force or entice
mothers to work if they
prefer to care for their
own children.

los problemas de salud,
educación, asistencia
social, y trabajo que
enfrentan estos niños
y sus familias.

La dirección de todo
programa -- sea para
el desarrollo del niño
o cuidar el niño --
tiene que estar en las
manos de los padres de
los niños en el
programa. De este modo
los padres de familia
como representantes de
la comunidad y los
barrios mantienen el
control y aseguran que
el ambiente del programa
refleja y respeta la
cultura, el idioma y
las costumbres del
niño. Servicios
tendran que ser sep-
arados de agencias de
Bienestar Público y
asegurar que madres
que prefieren cuidar
sus hijos no serán
obligadas de trabajar.

Through parliamentary error, the statement on
child care by the Black Caucus was not brought to
the floor for a vote by the delegates. It read:

We strongly urge that Federal funding be
available for Day Care Centers for all
children. Such programs should be
planned and directed by the people of
the community who use them and that this
funding not be through state or local
welfare agencies. All efforts to com-
mercialize Day Care centers should be
resisted.

The forum members support the thrust of this statement.

The statements by the Women's Caucus, and other
groups and forums, supporting universally available

developmental child care are also appreciated.
The full texts of these statements were not
available for detailed consideration by the forum
members at their final meeting.

SPECIAL RESOLUTIONS BY FORUM 17 MEMBERS

Forum 17 supported the convening of a plenary
session to deal with the following conflicts on a
conference-wide basis: direct delegate input to
the conference; racism; and neglect of chairmen and
vice chairmen in the initial planning of the
conference.

The forum panel also feels strongly that there
has been no convincing commitment of conference
officials or the Federal administration to sincerely act to implement the recommendations of the
conference. We urge the forum chairmen, vice
chairmen, and representatives of the conference
caucuses to remain an independent, self-constituted
body to continue to report to the delegates of the
White House conference and to the public on the
efforts or lack of efforts taken at the national
level to implement the forum's recommendations.

REFERENCES

1. Beatrice Rosenberg and Pearl G. Spindler,
    Day Care Facts, United States Department of
    Labor. Women's Bureau, Publication WB-70-213,
    May 1970, p. 1.

2. United States Department of Labor, Bureau of
    Labor Statistics. As presented in *Profiles of
    Children*, 1970 White House Conference on
    Children.

3. Mary Dublin Keyserling, *Working Mothers and
    the Need for Child Care Services*, United States
    Department of Labor, Women's Bureau, June
    1968, pp. 6-7.

4. Seth Low and Pearl G. Spindler, *Child Care
    Arrangements of Working Mothers in the United
    States*, Children's Bureau Publication No.
    461-1968, pp. 8-10.

5. See, for example, *Child Care Services Provided
    by Hospitals*, United States Department of
    Labor, Women's Bureau, Bulletin 295-1970,
    p. 20.

6. Low and Spindler, *op. cit.*, pp. 15-18.

7. Sixteen percent of all three- and four-year-
    olds in the United States, or 1.2 million
    children, now attend some form of educational
    nursery school, up from 9.6 percent in 1964.
    The increase is apparently largely the result
    of the Head Start Program. Data from the
    Census Bureau as reported in the *New York
    Times*, 11 October 1970, p. 8.

8. Mary Dublin Keyserling, *The Magnitude of Day
    Care Needs Today.* An address delivered to
    Forum 17 of the 1970 White House Conference
    on Children, 14 December, 1970. Reporting
    on preliminary results of "Windows on Day
    Care," report in preparation by the National
    Council of Jewish Women. Rosenberg and
    Spindler, *op. cit.*, p. 2.

9. Milton Willner, *The Magnitude and Scope of
    Family Day Care in New York City*, final
    report of Grant R120 from the Children's
    Bureau, 1966.

10. *Mental Health Services for Children*, prepared
    by the Center for Studies of Child and Family
    Mental Health, National Institute of Mental
    Health; Public Health Service publication 1844,
    October 1968.

11. *Crisis in Child Mental Health: Challenge for
    the 1970's*, Report of the Joint Commission on
    Mental Health of Children (New York: Harper &
    Row, 1969), p. 38.

12. President's Committee on Employment of the
    Handicapped, and National Institute of Child
    Health and Development. As presented in
    Profiles of Children, 1970 White House Con-
    ference on Children.

13. *Crisis in Mental Health*, *op. cit*, p. 27.

14. *Ibid.*, p. 62.

15. Rosenberg and Spindler, *op. cit.*, p. 27.

16. Keyserling, 1970, *op. cit.*

17. Florence A. Ruderman, "Conceptualizing Needs
    for Day Care," in *Day Care: An Expanding*

Resource for Children (New York Child Welfare League of America, 1965), pp. 14-27.

18.   Florence A. Ruderman, *Child Care and Working Mothers: A Study of Arrangements Made for Daytime Care of Children* (New York: Child Welfare League of America, 1968), pp. 88, 338-58.

19.   Lois M. Stolz, "Effects of Maternal Employ- ment in Children: Evidence of Research," *Child Development* 37 (1960): pp. 749-82.   See also F. I. Nye and Hoffman, *The Employed Mother in America* (Chicago: Rand McNally, 1963).

20.   Arthur C. Emlen, *Realistic Planning for the Day Care Consumer,* mimeograph, 1970.

21.   J. McV. Hunt, *Intelligence and Experience* (New York: Ronald, 1961); Benjamin S. Bloom, *Stability and Change in Human Characteristics* (New York: Wiley, 1964); Henry W. Maier, *Three Theories of Child Development: The Contributions of Erik H. Erikson, Jean Piaget, and Robert Sears, and their Applications* (New York: Harper & Row, 1965).

22.   *PCMR* Message.   "The Retarded Victims of Deprivation," an address by Whitney M. Young, Jr., Executive Director, National Urban League, to the 18th Annual Convention of the National Association for Retarded Children, Portland, Oregon,   19 October 1967 (Washington, D. C.:   The President's Committee on Mental Retardation, January 1968).

23.   Milton Willner, "Day Care; a Reassessment," *Child Welfare*   44 (1965):   pp. 125-133; World Health Organization, *Deprivation of Maternal Care: A Reassessment of its Effects* (Geneva: WHO).

24.   Bettye M. Caldwell and Lucille E. Smith, "Day Care for the Very Young -- Prime Opportunity for Primary Prevention," *American Journal of Public Health* 60 (1970):   pp. 690-97; Bettye M. Caldwell, Charlene M. Wright, Alice S. Honig, and Jordan Tannenbaum, "Infant Day Care and Attachment," *American Journal of Ortho- psychiatry* 40 (1970):   397-412.

25. See, for example, Joan W. Swift, "Effects of
     Early Group Experience: The Nursery School
     and Day Nursery," in *Review of Child Devel-
     opment Research*, ed. M. L. Hoffman and L. W.
     Hoffman (New York: Russell Sage, 1964),
     1: pp. 249-89.

26. Bettye M. Caldwell, "The Supportive Environ-
     ment Model of Early Enrichment," paper pre-
     sented at annual meeting of the American
     Psychological Association, Miami, Florida,
     September 1970; E. S. Schaefer, "Home Tutoring,
     Maternal Behavior and Infant Intellectual
     Development," paper presented at the American
     Psychological Association Meeting, Washington,
     D. C., September 1969; P. Levenstein, "Cogni-
     tive Growth in Preschoolers through Verbal
     Interaction with Mothers," *American Journal of
     Orthopsychiatry* 40 (1970): pp. 426-32; Laura L.
     Dittman, ed., *Early Child Care: The New
     Perspectives* (New York: Atherton, 1968).

27. Margaret Mead, "Some Theoretical Considerations
     on the Problem of Mother-child Separation,"
     American Journal of Orthopsychiatry 24 (1954):
     pp. 477.

28. Estimates of cost of care vary widely, depend-
     ing on the region of the country, age of the
     child, and type of care. The Office of Child
     Development has estimated for preschoolers
     that full-day center care ranges from $1245 to
     $2320 per child per year, for "minimal" from
     $1523 to $2372; for before and after school
     and summer care from $310 to $653. (*Standards
     and Costs for Day Care*, mimeograph of Office
     of Child Development, prepared by J. Sugarman,
     et al.) Additional breakdowns are given by
     R. Parker and J. Knitzer, *Background Paper on
     Day Care and Preschool Services: Trends in the
     Nineteen Sixties and Issues for the Nineteen
     Seventies*, prepared on behalf of the Office of
     Child Development for 1970 White House Con-
     ference on Children.

29. *Who are the Working Mothers?* Leaflet 37 (rev.),
     United States Department of Labor, Women's
     Bureau, May 1970.

30. For practical information on planning and
     operating developmental child care services,
     see the publications of the Child Development

Day Care Resources Project, jointly sponsored
by the United States Department of Health,
Education, and Welfare, Office of Child Development; the Office of Economic Opportunity;
and the Panel on Education Research and
Development of the President's Science Advisory Committee.   Ronald K. Parker, Project
Director.

31.   A. B. Willmon, "Parent Participation as a
Factor in the Effectiveness of Head Start
Programs," *Journal of Educational Research*
62 (1969): 406-10.

32.   Special thanks are due to the Forum 17 task
force on training and licensing, chaired by
June Sale, for many of the ideas on these
topics. Their full report will be made available at a later date.

33.   Special thanks are due to the Forum 17 task
force on delivery of services, chaired by Dr.
Alfred Kahn, for many of the ideas on this topic.
Their full report will be available at a later
date. The address of Wilbur Cohen to the forum
was also helpful in revising this and other
sections.

TASK FORCE ON DELIVERY OF SERVICES

Developmental Child Care Forum
White House Conference on Children 1970

TASK FORCE ASSIGNMENT

The Forum, as a whole, had a broad agenda and a tight
time table. The Task Force was therefore asked to explore
in more depth the service delivery aspects of the Forum
charge. The Task Force made a progress report to the
Forum, in the course of the White House Conference, and
benefited from discussion within the subunits of the
Forum. Some of our recommendations were enacted by the
Forum. Subsequently, meeting at the Conference and then

corresponding, the Task Force members amended the report.

TARGET

The Task Force defined as the target a comprehensive child care (day care) network, universally available, involving diverse facilities, and maximizing parental options.

A well-serviced community requires all-day care, part-day care, half-day care, after-school programs, family day care, "brief-time baby parking" facilities, and other program forms which will evolve. (Child care in the present sense, then, does not include 24-hour care or residential care.*) The evidence suggests that each of these program forms may be a superior choice for particular family and child situations. They should not, therefore, be listed in hierarchical order. Expression of preferences within the community and investigation of community situations and needs should make it possible to determine the optimum balance among the components such as these.

The legislative history of child care programs is that the Congress tends to prefer to enact categorical leglislation. There is no apparent inclination at the present time to develop a broadly designed, universally available program allowing substantial local options. It is therefore necessary, for those who are pointing towards a comprehensive network which maximizes choice, to develop administrative structures and delivery systems which will pull together the various categorical programs into the semblance of a network. Such pulling together also has the advantage of clarifying and defining gaps and pointing towards new

---

NOTE: We employ the term "child care" in present context, as it was utilized at the Conference to include day-time care and the associated educational, nutritional, health, social welfare and other activity focused on child development. Some of our members prefer "day care," reserving "child care" as a term for the broader child welfare and child development undertakings.

interim programs of the categorical type, which may be necessary as the network is gradually constructed.

The notion of a comprehensive child care network including a diversity of facilites imposes serious problems from the point of view of quality control. Criteria for quality control should be developed on the state and local level and must vary from program to program, since the length of exposure in the course of a day, the nature of the experience, and the goals will vary from program to program, too. It therefore becomes necessary to avoid imposing on program form A the quality control criteria relevant to program form B. This is a complex, unexplored issue; yet, if not recognized and coped with, this problem will inhibit development of the diverse program forms which are necessary.

It should also be clear that the pattern of funding, i.e., the basis for eligibility, does not determine just what type of program a given child needs. Similarly, auspices, manner of entry, and specific formulation of eligibility rules do not differentiate children as needing various components of custodial care, developmental stimulation, nutritional and health programs, social service support, all- or part-day schedules, group or family emphases, after-school programs, time with relatives.

Some of the programs mentioned can be quite expensive if they are undertaken on small scale. Thus, a family day care program, adequately serviced with nutritional, health, social service, and training supports can have a very large unit cost unless there is a considerable amount of family day care in the community, with various subunits sharing essential services which, in turn, are intensively used. The lesson, therefore, would appear to be that to create a comprehensive network involving a substantial number of diverse program forms is also to (a) undertake the elaboration of each of the program forms in sufficient quantity to achieve the elements of economy of scale appropriate to that form; or (see below) (b) to assure that daytime care programs share health, social services and related facilities which are established for general community purposes.

THE EMPHASIS ON CONSTRUCTING A SYSTEM

Although we begin with limited, quantitatively and qualitatively insufficient, and uneven categorical programs, the objectives cannot be achieved unless the emphasis will be upon the construction of a comprehensive system. Unless the diverse programs are in some formal relationship with one another, planned and coordinated by a body with some relationship to all of them, and are seen— in their totality—as having one task, the goals of this Forum and of this Task Force cannot be achieved. The notion of system is basic if there is ultimately to be coverage, access, coordination, the various points of entry, and equity.

One could begin de novo and design a system, but this would be artificial since many of the components are now with us and there has been some valuable constructive experience. One could merely repackage what we have, but the gaps and inadequacies would be considerable. The Task Force recommends a merging of these two approaches: repackaging what we have, but identifying and filling in gaps—as well as taking major new initiative.

This will not be achieved without an adequate planning and coordinating mechanism at each appropriate geographical governmental level, related to both political power and funding—an issue to be discussed subsequently.

Even though a given program may be categorical, the system itself should have sufficient power and be in a position to operate with sufficient ingenuity not only to maximize choice and assure access, not only to develop the necessary program mix, but also to provide for an appropriate mix of children from different social and economic backgrounds and to avoid segregation of children within programs on the basis of financial or other eligibility criteria. If there is a true system of services, there will obviously not be segregation by professional control, i.e. separation of programs by dominant profession. A system could be organized to clarify gaps, to monitor access, to avoid racial, ethnic, or economic segregation of children except insofar as positive identification leads some parent groups to seek it for their own purposes. Even in the latter instance, there are obviously problems to be faced.

The system in the sense here described is one that implements public responsibility. It cannot be achieved without public sanction. Therefore, it must obviously be public system. To say that the organization of the system and responsibility for it is public does not, of course, deny the likelihood that very large numbers of the program components will be under other than public auspices.

A DIVERSITY OF INSTRUMENTS

The Task Force believes that we will maximize diversity in program models, attractiveness to different population groups, innovation, flexibility and the possibility of parental input if a diversity of instruments is also accepted within the context of a publicly designated system. Thus, we would favor some combination of publicly operated programs, programs operated by the non-profit and profit components of the voluntary sector, programs operated locally by small proprietary groups ("mom and pop" centers), perhaps even programs operated on a franchise basis (see discussion below). In addition, we would give high priority to cooperatives created by parents who pool their entitlements.

With reference to the latter, we note that one of the most attractive forms of parental involvement in middle-class child care programs is found in parent-initiated cooperatives. Parents "pool" their tuition money and time to create a facility, making contributions of both in various combinations. Such models have much to contribute as new child care networks are created. Moreover, as parents in poverty communities and working-class communities achieve public entitlements, whether in the form of public payment of tuition, vouchers, or purchase of care, it would also be most appropriate for parents to pool such entitlements, and if the time permits, to share their own time as well to create new forms of cooperatives.*

The Task Force would stress a series of points about the various types of auspices mentioned above:

A. It is unacceptable that program emphasis should depend on auspice (which in turn relates to funding), i.e. that one program should be custodial, another developmental, etc. Children's needs and not auspice or funding pattern should determine program content. What is required everywhere is a developmental, not a custodial, emphasis.

B. Accountability is required, whatever the auspice of the program. This means licensing, inspection, reporting, assessment of effects.

C. Certain types of auspices by their nature preclude the availability of essential resources, i.e. nutrition services, health programs, mental health program, etc., unless they are tied into a larger service network. Therefore, when this is the case—as in the instance of family day care, small proprietary centers, cooperatives—it would be extremely important for the coordinating body responsible for the overall community system to organize and contract for specific services which might be shared among such facilities.

D. The Task Force is not encouraged by what it knows and can learn about franchise programs. Present evidence suggests that profit-making is possible in such operations only at the expense of program or

_____

*Apart from parent-operated cooperatives, parents might pool their entitlements and contract with a group to operate a program for them.

of limiting the service to more prosperous parents. Since the evidence is not complete and since such enterprises are not illegal, they obviously should not be closed out of the market. It is appropriate that they be required to meet local standards. On the other hand, the Task Force is not prepared to recommend that public funds be used to capitalize such operations.**

Finally, while we have emphasized the need to construct a system, we repeat that this does not preclude a variety of types of auspices for actual operations. A system is needed to assure mechanisms for relationships and accommodation, to provide for geographic coverage, reasonable eligibility standards, a variety of joint activities (intake, training, evaluation, shared services, etc.). Yet diverse auspices could offer choices to parents and provide necessary yardsticks. It may even be the case that the advantages of competition may come to be effective in this field. At the present time shortage of facilities and the existence of professional monopolies preclude real advantages from competition. Moreover, it is difficult for most parents, given their time and limited opportunity for observation, fully to evaluate the quality of the programs to which their children are exposed.

The validity of considerable parental participation in programs to assure responsiveness (see below) holds for all types of program forms. It would be appropriate, where public funds are at stake, to use such funding as a lever to strengthen parental roles in programs under all types of auspices.

ENTITLEMENTS

The goal already noted is day care and child development programs, universally available at parental option,

---

**One of our members distinguishes other proprietary from franchise operations and would not oppose employment of public funds to capitalize non-franchise proprietary centers.

offering a diversity of choices. At the present time, provision is best at either extreme of the economic scale, i.e., for those who can afford, at any price, to purchase good care for their children, and those who are eligible on a means test basis or because it opens the labor market to them. A variety of dilemmas are identified by the Task Force with relation to the question of entitlements.

First, there are those who would determine the priority of need with relation to an economic means test. The premise here is that parental option about the use of service is the critical issue and that people should be ranked in accord with whether they can most or least afford to provide the service for themselves. The alternate position says that, in setting priorities at a time that there are scarce resources, one should somehow rate parents by relative need for the service, economic issues aside. The Task Force sees validity in both of these approaches and believes that to make a choice between them is not good public policy at this time. However, since the latter approach involves the introduction of professional discretion and the minimization of parental option, we would in general favor an approach where the judgment about the need for services is made by parents and the ranking is made in terms of family means, if such a ranking indeed is essential. We urge that the supply of facilities be increased rapidly, so that such impossible choices should not have to be made very much longer.

We call special attention to the extreme "squeeze" experienced by the working poor and the lower middle class. Even the cheapest day care costs $1,000 a year. Facilities which offer a broader array of services range in cost from about $1,600 to about $3,200 or $3,300 per child per year. Such costs cannot be met by the working poor and lower middle class, and they tend, therefore, very frequently to "make do" with what are from any point of view unsatisfactory arrangements. Parents and children suffer because of such inadequacies, and the community ultimately pays for its deprivation and neglect. We would therefore urge that ways be found, in connection with pending legislation, to assure partial support for and partial meeting of the costs of services to the working poor and lower middle class who are now in such an economic squeeze. They should not have to devote an unreasonable portion of their incomes to child care. We note, too, that only such an approach will assure the socio-economic mix which we deem essential to the sound development of early childhood programs in all categories.

A final point needs to be made in this connection: income scales relating to the amount of payment to be made are not the same thing as income scales to determine eligibility. It may be reasonable to consider a mother's work income in examining the portion of the cost that she can bear, but it is certainly not reasonable to consider that income in determining whether she can have the child care upon which her going to work depends. Moreover, there are many people whose incomes more than justify waiving of all tuition for early childhood programs even though they are not eligible for public assistance.

THE QUESTION OF VOUCHERS

It has been proposed that, rather than operating public programs and making parents eligible for them, or purchasing care from programs in the voluntary sector on a contract basis, public authorities provide vouchers to parents who have a right to child care arrangements for their children, allowing the parents full opportunity to find and contract with the facility.

The objectives of the proponents of such proposals are praiseworthy: they would inspire competition among providers for the vouchers; they would increase parental option; they would mix within one facility people who enter via a variety of kinds of entitlements.

On the other hand, the voucher proposal is based on premises which do not at present obtain in the field here under discussion. If there is a shortage of facilities and a seller's market, a parent with a voucher does not actually enjoy any of the advantages of creating competition in providing service to him. Where there is a professional monopoly, as there is in such programs, the forces of the marketplace do not obtain in improving quality and lowering price. Where consumers are unsophisticated or lack access to information, or are not mobile, they do not become successful "shoppers" even if they have vouchers. One need merely examine the experience with Medicare or nursing homes generally to see the rationale for these concerns. Therefore, although the members of the Task Force would not oppose experiments with vouchers under controlled circumstances, where this may be possible, we would give higher priority to the employment of public funds to negotiate service contracts (and to permit competitive bidding among potential agencies for such contracts), and we would encourage also the use of the more traditional vendor payment approach. *Universalism* and *system* are key values which may not be consistent with widespread use of vouchers.

RESPONSIVENESS

Diversity, true parental choice and quality control all require, each in its own way, that there be built into the child care system provision to assure responsiveness of the system as a whole, and in its component parts, to consumers and to community objectives.

The Task Force places high priority on provision for parental control of the quality and character of programs through at least one-half of the places on the boards of *operating* centers at the local level. With reference to the area-wide body, we recognize that other elements in the community, apart from parents, have a very large stake in plans and program, and we endorse the notion of "community control," as requiring a minimum of one-third parent positions on the responsible bodies, and majority for members of the community as a whole. Area-wide bodies must concentrate on plans, priorities, monitoring, evaluation, budget allocation, coordination. Broad community representation makes it possible to plan over a larger time span and to introduce a broader perspective than may possible for parents whose children are currently in the centers.*

The majority of the members of the Task Force believe that parental control on the operating center level should include the hiring and firing of the center director. Sound administrative practice, however, also requires that the director himself have ultimate responsibility for hiring and firing other staff members. A minority of our group believes that parental control should extend to hiring and firing of other staff members as well, but this view would appear to the majority of the group to undermine administrative prerogatives. All members of the Task Force are in agreement, however, that there should be devices whereby parents can communicate to the director their responses to program and personnel, so that there may be alertness to

---

*One of our members sees this as a short-range issue. Given a goal of universality, he prefers a control structure like that for public schools. (Parents who want to buy privately, and can afford to do so, may.) In the long run, this new public institution will find a diversity of devices for parental "input," response, and contributions but will not seek parental "control" of operational units. He differentiates participation from control of a system which belongs to government (all the people), stressing responsive and responsible government.

Another member stresses local participation but considers a particular formula unrealistic since working parents have limited time.

A third believes that parents must be influential on the center board to affect and enrich program content as it touches their children but questions their ability to contribute to community-wide boards which must be concerned with planning, coordination, evaluation: "if two disparate levels of sophistication among participants are combined in one group, the less sophisticated are likely to be left . . . far behind . . . or it would be difficult to maintain the interest and participation of the others." At the very least, parents on area-wide boards would need technical staff help.

problems and difficulties. Parents under the several possible patterns obviously have a large role with reference to enrichment of program, assurance of an appropriate physical set up, determination of budget, and interpretation of program.

"Parents," in the present context, is read to mean *fathers* and *mothers*. In those child care programs involving children old enough to have policy or advisory role, i.e. particularly after-school programs, the latter, too, are regarded as important in determining the responsiveness of the total program. Places might be found for them on center and on area-wide boards. In general, attention must be directed to the problem of how representative consumers are to be selected for such committees and boards.

While the Task Force could not explore the matter in great detail, it calls attention to the fact that one aspect of responsiveness relates to the licensing and accreditation standards and procedures. In the past, these have been matters reserved largely for professional bodies or individual professionals. Mechanisms are being explored for a parental input, and the Task Force would encourage that such exploration be facilitated.

The kind of participation described should characterize individual centers as well as area-wide programs. We note, however, that there are parents whose life situation does not permit participation. Obviously, children in child care programs should not be penalized if parents will not or cannot participate. Children should not be excluded from programs if their parents are not in a position to make a personal commitment. The limiting case would be the situation in which parent cooperation is deemed essential to the child's adjustment in the program and is not forthcoming.

Since our proposals relate to a diversity of program forms, in communities with many types of tradition, and since we refer to parental groups whose life circumstances may in various ways impede the kind of participation discussed, the Task Force recommends that the proposals above be regarded as goals. Certainly, the goal of parental representation as constituting at least half of the governing boards of operating centers under public auspices is an immediate and feasible one in most localities.*

COORDINATION AND PLANNING

A variety of major problems face early childhood programs in many parts of the country. Programs are categorical, and operations are therefore fragmented. The administrative fragmentation complicates the situation in dealing with personnel on state and federal levels. Paper work is excessive and requirements are sometimes contradictory. Major bottlenecks appear in the distribution of funds and make it difficult to meet commitments and retain staff. Rules and regulations as well as procedures quite often make it difficult to be responsive to parental circumstances at the local level and to the specific needs of children. Sometimes, intervening levels try to block programs supported by higher levels and planned by groups responsible for centers. Full resolution of such difficulties will demand comprehensive assessment and a variety of administrative and legislative reforms. For the present, the Task Force would emphasize the need for two levels of planning and coordinating provisions:

1. At the "higher" or "larger" geographic level, there is need for an instrument (either state-wide, area-wide, regional, or large-city) which will allocate resources, give technical aid, promote programs, certify communities as meeting minimum standards, and assess community plans. We are not prepared at the moment to indicate what the exact level should be at which the above instrument is located,

---

*Opposing a fixed formula, one of our members argues that "most working mothers have too much to do to be actively involved in a board."

recognizing as we do that there is a major reexamination of the components of the federal system. There are forces which would place the "action" in regional offices, in self-organized clusters of states, at the state level, just as there are those who would place emphasis on standard metropolitan statistical areas, or large cities as the units which would negotiate with the federal structure.

2. Whatever the identity of the higher-level organization, there is needed at the local level (medium-size city, town, village, county, or portion of large city) an instrument to funnel the major streams of funds for early childhood programs, to serve as liaison with the higher level when statutes block implementation, to formulate and adopt local standards, to approve plans submitted by specific facilities, and—most important—to take responsibility for shaping the several components into the kind of system described above. This local instrument should be chosen by and be responsible to the executive branch of government, since it must relate to the budgeting process and to formal planning procedures and instruments. As already indicated, the components of parent and community representation on advisory or policy committees—depending on local practice—should be considerable. Such local instrument should have responsibility for consumer education, i.e., to increase the sophistication of potential users of such programs.

It would appear clear, from the description of the planning and coordination requirements of early child care programs, that although the program called Community Coordinated Child Care (4-C Program) is evolving on the basis of community experience with coordination, and may change its name and guidelines, the basic 4-C concept should very much be built into the planning and coordinating structure of the ongoing program. Otherwise, the lack of continuity will do much to disorganize child care programs throughout the country.

SPECIAL PROBLEMS IN RURAL AREAS

Although our exploration of the subject was limited, we should like to underscore the special problems of child care systems in rural areas. Where populations are spread far apart, group day care may not be possible, and family-based programs may have higher priority. Under such circumstances, specialists such as nutrition experts, health personnel, etc., may be used to "ride circuit" to enrich the program.

By their nature, such programs require a rather high investment in transportation, since some children may have to travel as much as 15 or 20 miles. This must be taken into account in the funding patterns.

Thus, a point made earlier with reference to such programs as family day care and small proprietary programs in urban areas becomes doubly important in rural areas: there must be experimentation with and investment in the development of central services to enrich programs in ways which are not possible for the operating unit. Specific guidelines and aids are needed in this general field.

LICENSING AND STANDARD SETTING

These topics merit specific and intensive investigation. There is great confusion in the field about these subjects, and the implementation of both licensing and standard setting throughout the country imposes unmanageable hurdles on the one hand, and misses opportunities for the protection of children on the other.

Licensing relates to the use of police power for protective purposes, i.e., meeting of fire codes, safety standards, building appropriateness. Standard setting offers positive guidance in various ways. Where standards are met, the program may be fully accredited.

There was some feeling within the group, although the subject was not adequately explored, that for places which do not require licensing in this field, the federal government, through its funding mechanisms, should set minimum protective standards. However, it should be willing to let states and localities take over when they are prepared to go beyond this. It is urgent that the federal government avoid unrealistic standards or seek uniformity within what must and should be regional diversity.

If localities and states are to make progress in this area, they will need some financial support to assist them. Funding arrangements under the several federal programs should make budgetary provision for work on licensing and standards. There should also be provision for adequate training for such functions. The suggestion was made that resources could become available if licensing and standard-setting could be viewed as a service, rather than as an administrative function. As a service, licensing could be understood in its positive sense and become eligible for federal fund-matching (75 percent as a regular service or 90 percent federal funding if a mandatory supportive service). Should federal funding become available, the training of licensing staff would be possible and, indeed, might be mandated.

Where exceptions to requirements are offered to permit the active development of programs and necessary coverage, there should be clear timetables and target dates for the meeting of standards so that children may be adequately protected and their development enhanced.

HEALTH PROGRAMS, NUTRITION, SOCIAL SERVICES

These topics are the subject of a variety of reports deriving from Head Start, day care and other programs. One of the main contributions of child care programs is the assurance that children in need of such services as can be rendered by doctors, dentists, and nutritionists should have access to them. Families requiring other kinds of social services should, of course, be brought into contact with such programs and given access to the help they need.

This much said, we would note that it would hardly be wise for the child care system to seek to develop independent programs in all these fields. Indeed, families are not well served if fragmentation is increased. What the community needs is an integrated social service system, with provision for coverage, continuity of care, and case accountability. What the system of child care services requires is adequate provision for case finding, referral, case integration. Children and families should be channeled to the more specialized facilities. Thus, where the community has health and dental services, obviously the children in the programs should use such services. This would be far wiser than to create new services built into the child care programs. On the other hand, we note that there are certain service program specifics which are essential to the very quality of the child care programs and germane to the experience. These should be administratively built into and related to such programs. We believe that nutrition programs are in such category. Early childhood programs should also have social service aides or social workers for those social service activities which relate to the ongoing program itself. For other purposes, these social workers and aides may be seen as case finders who will make referrals and assure contact with other components of the community social service system.

We wish in short to assure the enrichment of the program, the continuity of the program, but also that the program become an opportunity for case finding and for bringing concrete services to children and their families.

SOME MAJOR POINTS REVIEWED

1. The goal recommended is a universal child care system, with service available as a right to all parents and

children, and structured so as to reflect diverse needs and to maximize individual choice.

2. Given ultimate costs, manpower requirements, and time involved in developing programs, we recognize that the system must evolve in stages; but it should be defined as a target now.

3. Categorical programs which now exist should be administratively interrelated at both planning and delivery levels to create the outlines of the system and to identify gaps.

4. A system must include and encourage development of diverse program forms: group care, all-day care, part-day care, after-school care, family day care, and so on.

5. Quality control appropriate to each form should be sought. Professionals, parents, and community members should be involved in the definition of quality control standards for each form.

6. The system, based on public responsibility and accountability, may include at the delivery level: publicly operated programs; programs operated by the non-profit voluntary sector; programs operated on a proprietary basis; franchise programs (if chosen by parents for their individual children on the basis of their individual entitlements, but not to be publicly capitalized or used as the major public instrument).

7. To reflect parental and child needs, the system must be organized for maximal responsiveness. Parents should constitute at least a majority of the board of local-level operating program units. They must also constitute a significant portion (at least one-third) of boards responsible for community-wide planning and coordination. Center boards should have the right to hire and fire center directors. They should be involved in the process but not control the process in relation to other staff members, who are directly responsible to the center director.

8. To plan, update and to implement a comprehensive child care system, there must be developed for each large jurisdiction (a choice will need to be made among state,

region, standard metropolitan statistical area, etc.) a planning and coordinating mechanism concerned with fund allocation to sub-areas, overall planning, setting the basic minimum standards, creation of central services and technical assistance, encouraging and inspiring local groups to create coordinating mechanisms and to implement programs. On the direct operating level, a coordinating-planning mechanism which will not itself operate programs, should be developed for city, county, large neighborhood area, or district to allocate local funds assigned by the higher level, to develop locally specific standards, to provide central services and technical assistance, to offer seed money to new units, to coordinate, to initiate and to assure sponsorship for new programs. This latter mechanism is seen as evolving from and incorporating the knowledge and experience of successful 4-C programs, but placing such activity on a local statutory basis.

PARTICIPANTS

Jeannette L. Burroughs
Rehable M. Edwards
Florence B. Falk
Norman S. Finkel
Alfred J. Kahn, CHAIRMAN
Ferne K. Kolodner
Trude W. Lash
Irving Lazar
Evelyn Linder
Norman V. Lourie
Maureen McKinley
Gwen Morgan
Jeanne Mueller
Elizabeth Prescott
Thomas Rosica
Dorothy Stevenson
Herman Wilson
Julianne Zuck

SELECTED RESOURCES FOR ADDITIONAL INFORMATION*

Appalachian Regional Commission
1666 Connecticut Avenue, N.W.
Washington, D.C. 20235

Association for Childhood Education International
3615 Wisconsin Avenue, N.W.
Washington, D.C. 20016

Child Welfare League of America
67 Irving Pl.
New York, New York 10003

Day Care Council of America
1401 K Street, N.W.
Washington, D.C. 20005

ERIC Clearinghouse on Early Childhood
National Laboratory on Early Childhood Education
805 West Pennsylvania Avenue
Urbana, Illinois 61801

National Association for the Education of Young Children
1834 Connecticut Avenue, N.W.
Washington, D.C. 20009

National Council of Organizations for Children and Youth
1910 K Street, N.W.
Washington, D.C. 20006

National Education Association
1201 16th Street, N.W.
Washington, D.C. 20036

Office of Child Development
Department of Health, Education and Welfare
Washington, D.C. 20201

United States Office of Education
Department of Health, Education and Welfare
Washington, D.C. 20201

Women's Bureau
United States Department of Labor
Washington, D.C. 20210

* Publications, research reports and additional resources can be
obtained from these organizations. Additional references and resources
will be contained in subsequent volumes of *Child Care: A Comprehensive
Guide.*

BIBLIOGRAPHY

ABT Associates, Inc. *A study in child care.* 4 Vols. Washington, D.C.: Office of Economic Opportunity, 1971.

Adair, T. & Eckstein, E. *Parents and the day care center.* N.Y.: Federation of Protestant Welfare Agencies, Inc., 1961.

American Academy of Pediatrics, Committee on the Infant and Pre-School Child. *Recommendations for day care centers for infants and children.* Evanston, Ill.: American Academy of Pediatrics, 1973.

Auerbach-Fink, S. *Parents and child care: a report on child care consumers in San Francisco: a study of parental expectations for child care services from a cross-cultural perspective.* San Francisco: Far West Laboratory, 1974.

Barclay, D. The tangled case of the working mother. *The New York Times Magazine,* May 14, 1961.

Beer, E. Working mothers and the day nursery. N.Y.: Whiteside, Inc., 1957.

Biber, B. *Challenges ahead for early childhood education.* Washington, D.C.: National Association for the Education of Young Children, 1969.

Boguslowski, D. B. *Guide for establishing and operating day care centers for young children.* N.Y.: Child Welfare League of America, Inc., 1970.

Bowlby, J. *Attachment and loss.* Vol. 1. N.Y.: Basic Books, 1969.

Breitbart, V. *The day care book: the why, what and how of community day care.* N.Y.: Alfred A. Knopf, 1974.

Bronfenbrenner, U. *Day care U.S.A.: a statement of principles.* Washington, D.C.: U.S. Department of Health, Education and Welfare, Office of Child Development, 1970.

Butler, A. L. *Current research in early childhood education: a compilation and analysis for program planners.* Washington, D.C.: NEA American Association of

Elementary Kindergarten and Nursery Educators, 1970.

Caldwell, B. M. *Educational day care for infants and young children.* N.Y.: Holt, Rinehart and Winston, 1971.

Caldwell, B. M. A timid giant grows bolder. *Saturday Review.* Feb. 20, 1971.

Cauman, J. *Family day care and group day care, to essential aspects.* N.Y.: Child Welfare League, 1961.

Cauman, J. (Ed.) *Day care: an expanding resource for children.* study of day care: Washington, D.C.

Center for The Study of Public Policy. *Feasibility report and design of an impact study of day care: final report February, 1971.* Washington, D.C.: Office of Economic Opportunity, 1971.

Cohen, M. D. (Ed.) *Help for day care workers.* Washington, D.C.: Association for Childhood Education International, 1971.

Crisis in child mental health: challenge for the 1970's: report of the Joint Commission on Mental Health of Children. N.Y.: Harper and Row, 1969.

Day care licensing study: summary report on phase I: state and local day care requirements. Washington, D.C.: U.S Department of Health, Education and Welfare, 1973.

Developmental child care services. Report of Forum 17. Washington, D.C.: White House Conference on Children, 1970.

Ditmore, J. & Prosser, W. R. *A study on day care's effects on the labor force participation of low income mothers.* Washington, D.C.: Office of Economic Opportunity, 1973.

Dittman, L. L. (Ed.) *Early child care: the new perspectives.* N.Y.: Atherton Press, 1968.

Dittman, L. *Children in day care.* Washington, D.C.: U.S. Department of Health, Education and Welfare, The Children's Bureau, No. 444, 1967.

Early childhood education: report of the Task Force on Early

Childhood Education. Sacramento, Ca.: State Department of Early Education, 1972.

Education Commission of the States. *Early childhood development: alternatives for program implementation in the states.* Denver: Education Commission of the States, 1971.

Education Commission of the States. *A handbook for gathering data and assessing needs.* Denver: Education Commission of the States, 1973.

Education Commission of the States. *Establishing a state office of early childhood development.* Denver: Education Commission of the States, 1972.

Evans, E. B., Shub, B., & Weinstein, M. *Day care: how to plan, develop and operate a day care center.* Boston: Beacon Press, 1971.

Fein, G. & Clarke-Stewart, A. *Day care in context.* N.Y.: John Wiley and Sons, 1973.

Ford, S. P. *Guidelines for day care services.* N.Y.: Child Welfare League, 1972.

Gilfillan, V. G. *Day care as a therapeutic service to preschool children and its potential as a preventative service.* Child Welfare League, 1962.

Run a day care service. N.Y.: Day Care Council of New York, 1971.

Heinicke, C. M., Friedman, D., Prescott, E., Puncel, C., & Sole, J. S. The organization of day care—considerations relating to the mental health of child and family. *American Journal of Orthopsychiatry,* Jan. 1973, **43**(1).

Hess, R. Parent training programs and community involvement in day care in E. H. Grotberg (Ed.), *Day care: resources for decisions.* Washington, D.C.: Office of Economic Opportunity, 1971.

Herzog, E. *Children of working mothers.* Washington, D.C.: U.S. Department of Health, Education and Welfare, Children's Bureau, Social and Rehabilitation Service, 1960.

Keyserling, M. D. *Windows on day care: a report based on findings of the National Council of Jewish Women.* N.Y.: The National Council of Jewish Women, 1972.

Hoffman, L. W. Effects of the maternal employment on the child. *Child Development,* 1961.

Industry and day care: report of the First Conference on Industry and Day Care. Chicago: Urban Research Corp., 1970.

Mayer, A. B. & Kahn, A. J. *Day care as a social instrument.* N.Y.: Columbia University School of Social Work, 1965.

Meade, M. The politics of day care. *Commonweal,* April 10, 1971.

Nixon, R. Veto of economic opportunity amendments of 1971. *Weekly Compilation of Presidential Documents.* Washington, D.C.: U.S. Government Printing Office, December 13, 1971.

Perspectives on Child Care In Harvard Center for Law and Education. *Inequality in Education.* Washington, D.C.: National Association for the Education of Young Children, No. 13, Dec. 1972.

Peters, A. D. Day care—a summary report. *American Journal of Public Health,* 1964.

Prescott, E. *A pilot study of day care centers and their clientele.* Washington, D.C.: U.S. Education and Welfare, Education and Welfare, Children's Bureau, No. No. 428, 1965.

Rivlin, Day Care and Child Development Council of America, 1973.

Ratliff, P. *Organizing to coordinate child care services.* Washington, D.C.

Roby, P. *Child care–who cares? Foreign and domestic infant and early childhood development policies.* N.Y.: Basic Books, 1973.

Sidel, R. *Women and child care in China: a first hand report.* N.Y.: Hill and Wang, 1972.

Siegel, A. *Research issues related to the effects of maternal employment on children.* University Park, Md.: Social Science Research Center, 1961.

Seigel, A. E. & Haas, M. B. *The working mother: a review of research child development.* 1963.

Steiner, G. Y. *The state of welfare.* Washington, D.C.: The Brookings Institute, 1971.

Steinfels, M. *Who's minding the children? The history and politics of day care in America.* N.Y.: Simon and Schuster, 1973.

Stoltz, L. M. Effects of maternal employment on children. *Child Development.* 1960.

U.S. Congress, H.R. 6848. *A Bill to Provide a Comprehensive Child Development Act.* 92nd Congress, 1st session, 1971.

U.S. Congress. *Economic Opportunity Amendments of 1971, Conference Report.* 92nd Congress, 1st session, Report No. 92-682, 1971.

U.S. Congress, House Select Subcommittee on Education, Committee on Education and Labor. *Comprehensive Preschool and Child Day Care Act of 1969: Hearings on H.R. 13520.* 91st Congress, 1st and 2nd sessions, 1969 and 1970.

U.S. Congress, Senate Committee on Finance. *Material related to child care legislation: description of S.2003.* 92nd Congress, 1st session, 1971.

U.S. Congress, Senate Committee on Finance. *Child Care Hearings on Child Care: Provision of H.R. 1,* Sept. 22-24, 1971.

U.S. Congress, Senate Committee on Finance. *Child care: data and materials.* 92nd Congress, 1st session, June 16, 1971.

U.S. Congress, Senate Committee on Finance. *Child care legislation.* 92nd Congress, 1st session, July 23, 1971.

U.S. Congress, Senate Committee on Finance. *Additional material related to child care legislation.* 92nd Congress, 1st session, Sept. 21, 1971.

U.S. Congress, Senate Subcommittee on Children and

Youth, Committee on Labor and Public Welfare. *American families: trends and pressures.* Hearings held Sept. 24-26, 1973.

U.S. Department of Health, Education and Welfare. *Proceedings of the National Conference on Day Care Services,* May 13-15, 1965. Washington, D.C. The Children's Bureau Publication No. 438. 1966.

U.S. Department of Labor. *Day care services: industry's involvement.* Washington, D.C.: The Department of Labor Women's Bureau, Bulletin No. 296, 1971.

Westinghouse Learning Corp. & Westat Research Inc. *Day care survey 1970.* Washington, D.C.: Office of Economic Opportunity, April 1971.

White, S. *Federal programs for young children: review and recommendations.* 4 Vols. Cambridge, Mass.: The Huron Institute for U.S. Department of Health, Education and Welfare, Sept. 1972.

World Health Organization. *Care of children in day care centers.* Geneva, Public Health Papers, No. 24, 1964.

Zamoff, R. B. *Guide to assessment of day care services and needs at the community level.* Washington, D.C.: The Urban Institute, 1971.

INDEX